LEADING
MATTERS

John L. Hennessy

LEADING
MATTERS

Lessons from My Journey

STANFORD BUSINESS BOOKS
AN IMPRINT OF STANFORD UNIVERSITY PRESS
STANFORD, CALIFORNIA

Stanford University Press

Stanford, California

Special discounts for bulk quantities of Stanford Business Books are available to corporations, professional associations, and other organizations. For details and discount information, contact the special sales department of Stanford University Press. Tel: (650) 725-0820, Fax: (650) 725-3457

Printed in the United States of America on acid-free, archival-quality paper

Library of Congress Cataloging-in-Publication Data

Names: Hennessy, John L., author.
Title: Leading matters : lessons from my journey / John L. Hennessy.
Description: Stanford, California : Stanford Business Books, an imprint of Stanford University Press, 2018. | Includes bibliographical references and index.
Identifiers: LCCN 2018009505 | ISBN 9781503608016 (cloth : alk. paper) | ISBN 9781503608023 (epub)
Subjects: LCSH: Leadership—United States. | Hennessy, John L. | College administrators—United States—Biography. | Businessmen—United States—Biography. | Stanford University—Biography.
Classification: LCC HD57.7 .H4457 2018 | DDC 658.4/092—dc23
LC record available at https://lccn.loc.gov/2018009505

Cover design by Rob Ehle
Text design by Bruce Lundquist
Typeset at Stanford University Press in 11.5/16 Baskerville

To Andrea,
my life partner for the past forty-eight years
and my companion on these journeys

CONTENTS

Foreword by Walter Isaacson   ix

Introduction   1

1. Humility: The Basis for Effective Leadership   9

2. Authenticity and Trust: The Essential Ingredients
   for Effective Leadership   21

3. Leadership as Service: Understanding Who Works
   for Whom   35

4. Empathy: How It Shapes a Leader and an Institution   51

5. Courage: Standing Up for the Institution and
   the Community   65

6. Collaboration and Teamwork: You Cannot Do It Alone   83

7. Innovation: The Key to Success in Industry and Academia   101

8. Intellectual Curiosity: Why Being a Lifelong Learner
   Is Crucial   117

9. Storytelling: Communicating a Vision   127

10. Legacy: What You Leave Behind   139

   Conclusion: Building the Future   153

   Coda: Books from Which I Have Learned   159

Acknowledgments   177

Notes   179

Index   181

FOREWORD

Walter Isaacson

The biggest regret you will feel when finishing this book is that you didn't read it earlier. All of us who have struggled to be good leaders would have found our way more easily if our paths had been lit by this wonderful guide.

John Hennessy has been one of the most creative leaders of our time, combining intellect with wisdom. As Stanford University's president, he was a great manager and executive as well as a visionary. In addition, he has mentored and molded scores of other great leaders. So he has a deep understanding of the components of leadership.

There is no one formula for being a great leader. Take America's founders, for example. Some were men of great intellectual vision, such as Jefferson and Madison. Others had great passion, like John Adams and his cousin Samuel. Washington's foremost traits were his rectitude, gravitas, and commanding presence. And then there were leaders like Benjamin Franklin, whose sage manner and humor could bring strong personalities together and get them to collaborate and compromise.

Through his own experience and from watching others, Hennessy draws lessons from various leadership styles and is able to distill ten core concepts. They are presented in this book not simply as abstract principles but with insightful stories and memorable anecdotes that bring them to life.

He begins with humility, which is fitting because that is a quality that is most evident and surprising in himself. Both in person and in this book, Hennessy exudes the strength that comes from confidence but also the openness that comes with the true humility of wanting to appreciate the opinions of others.

We often think great leaders need to be driven by unwavering conviction and willing to ignore second-guessers. We think they need to have a healthy ego. In fact, however, the worst combination for a leader is to combine ego and insecurity, as happens too often, especially in politics. Both in this book and in his life, Hennessy shows how the recipe for great leadership is the opposite: being secure yet humble.

Two of the people I have written about—Albert Einstein and Steve Jobs—were not known for being humble. But in fact they each had a deep inner humility. For Einstein, it stemmed from the awe he felt for the beauty of nature's laws. When a sixth-grade girl from New York wrote to ask about his religious feelings, he replied, "There is a spirit manifest in the laws of the universe—a spirit vastly superior to that of humankind—in the face of which we must feel very humble." For Jobs, who was deeply spiritual, his Buddhist training did not rid him of his surface brashness and occasional aggressiveness, but he listened intently and fully processed the opinions of others.

Benjamin Franklin once said that he was never able to master the virtue of humility, but he learned the pretense of humility—he knew that feigning it was useful in dealing with others. That would seem to defy Hennessy's second principle of leadership, which is to be authentic. Franklin, however, goes on to teach us, as does Shakespeare's Prince Hal, that we become the mask we wear. In other words, when we have difficulty in mastering a virtue, it sometimes helps to display it nonetheless, and over time we will be able to internalize it. I personally found that true for another of Hennessy's leadership skills, courage. As a leader of journalistic enterprises, I was often afraid to take risks, but by putting on a front of fearlessness at important moments I learned how to be actually more courageous.

Humility forms the foundation for many of the other principles that Hennessy describes, such as empathy and regarding leadership as service. It is especially relevant for one of the key concepts in this book, which is the importance of collaboration. As Franklin explained in his autobiography, displaying and then learning humility caused him to listen to other people, help them find common ground, and get them to work together. The four seminal innovations of the digital age—the transistor, computer, microchip, and packet-switched network—were all developed by collaborative teams rather than singular inventors. When I asked Steve Jobs what his greatest product was, he did not say the Macintosh or the iPhone, but instead simply said, "the team at Apple."

Hennessy also explores the virtue of curiosity, which is a trait that was exemplified by my latest biography's subject, Leonardo da Vinci. Da Vinci had an insatiable drive to learn everything possible about everything that was knowable. With a passion both playful and obsessive, he pursued studies of anatomy, fossils, art, architecture, music, birds, the heart, flying machines, optics, botany, geology, water flows, and weaponry. It allowed him to fathom how the "infinite works of nature," as he put it, are woven together in a unity filled with marvelous patterns. His ability to combine art and science, made iconic by his drawing of a perfectly proportioned man spread-eagled inside a circle and square, known as Vitruvian Man, made him history's most creative genius. That trait of wide-ranging curiosity is one that distinguishes the truly creative leaders of our time as well, including Steve Jobs, Bill Gates, Jeff Bezos, and John Hennessy.

There is one leadership skill in this book that I found a bit unexpected but also profound: storytelling. One of my early mentors, the novelist Walker Percy, told me when I left our home state to become a journalist in New York, "There are two types of people who come out of Louisiana, preachers and storytellers. Be a storyteller, because the world already has too many preachers." That is the joy of Hennessy's book. It is filled with lessons, but he conveys them through stories. He understands that leadership is about creating a narrative. If you know how to tell the stories, you will be able to shape the narrative.

.   .   .

Walter Isaacson is a professor of history at Tulane University. He was formerly the CEO of the Aspen Institute, editor of *Time* magazine, and chair of CNN. His books include *The Innovators* and biographies of Benjamin Franklin, Albert Einstein, Steve Jobs, and Leonardo da Vinci.

LEADING
MATTERS

INTRODUCTION

"Regard your good name as the richest jewel you can possibly be
possessed of—for credit is like fire; when once you have kindled it you
may easily preserve it, but if you once extinguish it, you will find it an
arduous task to rekindle it again. The way to a good reputation is to
endeavor to be what you desire to appear."
Popularly attributed to Socrates (no definitive source)

Few of us live our lives exactly the way we planned. If we're fortunate, that can be a good thing. Certainly that has been true for me.

In one respect, I have lived my dream. I am still married to my high school sweetheart, Andrea. We have two wonderful sons. I have spent much of my life working in the field of computing, a passion I developed while still in high school, and I have been a professor for forty years at one of the greatest universities in the world, a career I set my sights on when I was an undergraduate.

When I was offered a position as assistant professor in the Department of Electrical Engineering at Stanford, at the age of twenty-five, it was a dream come true. I accepted the offer on the spot (although it was not the best salary offer I received). Choosing my spouse and saying yes to that offer were the two best decisions of my life (in that order).

If, back then, you had asked me my plans, I would have told you that I wished to spend my life exactly where I was, retiring decades in the future, perhaps with some teaching and research awards, some important published papers, perhaps a patent or two, and the title of emeritus.

It was a lovely dream, and I suspect I would have been happy pursuing it. Indeed, forty years later I still love being in the classroom or engaging in an energetic discussion about research. But, as they say, stuff happens. An unplanned and unexpected step, becoming an entrepreneur, took my journey in a different direction, eventually delivering me to the series of leadership positions I have held over the past twenty-five years.

This book is about the lessons I learned along the way, both during my early years as a professor and then as an entrepreneur, but mostly throughout that twenty-five-year leadership journey. These stories recount what worked, and sometimes didn't work, for me. While a few of the lessons apply most directly either to industry or to the academic and nonprofit worlds, aspects of each prove relevant either way. Similarly, while my experiences range from being a first-level leader to leading an entire institution, most of what I have learned applies to any level of leadership. Yes, the crises get bigger and come faster when you are at the top of a large organization, but the problems, and how they could be best confronted, are similar.

As Walter Isaacson says in the Foreword, "There is no one formula for being a great leader." Nor do I believe there are many dictates, beyond the obvious and conventional ones. Instead, I offer my thoughts about ten elements of leadership that shaped my journey, along with a set of stories about how I relied on these traits in pivotal moments. I hope others find these reflections helpful in their own leadership journeys.

Before diving in, I want to offer a little more background. I came to Stanford in 1977, a time when Silicon Valley and the information age were young. Apple was only a year old; Intel was still a modest-sized company making primarily memory chips. Personal computers, the Internet, the World Wide Web, and cellular phones had not yet been invented. I began my career teaching and doing research with a focus on Very Large Scale Integration (VLSI) and the emergence of microprocessors. Although I had some early involvement in two start-ups—most important, Jim Clark's company, Silicon Graphics—my attention was overwhelmingly focused on my Stanford career.

As described in Chapter 2, "Authenticity and Trust," the key step that changed my career trajectory was cofounding a company (MIPS Computer Systems) based on the research I had undertaken at Stanford between 1981 and 1984. During a leave from the university, I gave my primary attention to that company, and even after returning from that leave, the company took up a considerable amount of my consulting time and summers. Although I flirted several times with the idea of remaining at MIPS, I really missed working with the students, both in the classroom and in research, so I made Stanford my primary home once again.

The five years that passed from the time we founded MIPS until its successful IPO changed me. Having faced several crises in the company, I felt better positioned to handle such challenges. Furthermore, having seen how a small, determined team could change the world by starting something new, I was ambitious to see my department, my school (engineering), and my university make a bigger and more positive impact in the world. I could have returned to simply being a professor: in my view, there is no more noble or rewarding career for an individual contributor. Instead I embarked on what would become a leadership journey of twenty-plus years.

Initially, the leadership demands were modest: I was director of Stanford's Computer System Laboratory, an interdisciplinary laboratory of about fifteen faculty members in computer science and electrical engineering. There I enjoyed helping find and recruit great new colleagues, as well as mentoring and supporting them as they began their Stanford careers. In 1994, I was asked to chair Stanford's Computer Science Department, but I still managed to teach and lead a research group doing exciting work.

Two years later, I was named dean of the School of Engineering. The job was much bigger: two-hundred-plus faculty members instead of thirty-five, but my colleagues were all engineers. We spoke a common vocabulary and had similar measures of success. I loved that job. My wife still insists it was the best job of the many I have held. Why? Well, I could know all the faculty in the school, have some idea of what their research was about, individually greet and welcome every new professor we hired, and still teach a course every year and advise a few PhD students.

All of that changed three years later, in 1999, when Stanford president Gerhard Casper asked me to succeed Condoleezza Rice as provost, the equivalent of chief operating officer of the university. I was astonished—and a bit worried. As you will see, accepting that job was a big step.

A few months later, to my surprise, President Casper announced his intention to resign at the end of the academic year that was just starting. I had taken the job to work closely with President Casper, to focus on big institutional challenges, and as an opportunity to learn about my colleagues outside of engineering. In truth, I was still learning the ropes of a challenging new post. Nonetheless, after an extensive search process running from October to March, and many meetings with search committee members, the board of trustees asked me to become Stanford's tenth president, starting in the fall of 2000.

Despite the vetting process, I was somewhat amazed—and more than a little afraid. I was only forty-seven, my experiences as a senior executive in a large institution were brief, and my knowledge of navigating a vast bureaucracy was limited. I worried that I would disappoint everyone. Yet I was attracted by the challenge of enhancing an institution that had done so much for me. I hoped that I could succeed, if I approached the job with humility about my own skills, a scientist's respect for the facts, and a stellar team.

While I had my experience from Silicon Valley and a set of colleagues at Stanford, whom I regarded as friends, other than President Casper and a few members of the board of trustees, I did not have many senior people to look toward for advice. So, like any good researcher, I began reading books on leadership, especially biographies of great leaders: how they developed, how they worked with others, and how they overcame adversity. (You'll see a list of those books in the Coda.) I also resolved to stay intellectually curious and to expand my interests beyond science and technology to encompass the humanities, the social sciences, medicine, and the arts.

Did I succeed as a university president? Did I become a great leader along the way? Did our team make a great university even better? That's not for me to decide. The metric that the provost, John Etchemendy, and I thought was most important for measuring our success was the quality of the people, the faculty and students that are the university. That's difficult to measure, compared to simpler metrics such as facilities built or dollars raised. At the end of my tenure as president in August 2016, by most measures of the faculty and student quality (for example, rankings, selectivity, and yield), Stanford was a match for the best universities in the world. In addition, we had established a leadership position in multidisciplinary research and teaching, a goal the provost and I had embraced early in our terms (see Chapter 7, "Innovation"). The longevity of our joint tenure—sixteen years, or roughly double the national average for university presidents—was key to what we accomplished.

By all rights, the story might have ended there. What could I possibly do that could be even a fraction as challenging and impactful as running Stanford University? I sat on the boards of Google, Cisco, and several important foundations. Surely that work, plus perhaps teaching a few courses, would be a fitting conclusion to my somewhat unexpected career.

That's when the most extraordinary thing happened: a musing of mine about the need to train the next generation of the world's leaders was suddenly realized with the help of one of America's great business leaders, Phil Knight, the founder of Nike. Together we would launch the Knight-Hennessy Scholars program, the most ambitious undertaking of its kind since the Rhodes Scholars began more than a century ago.

The Knight-Hennessy Scholars program brought me back to my roots as a faculty member and an entrepreneur: starting a program from scratch and wondering what exactly we should teach a group of brilliant young scholars, if we were to prepare them to be future global leaders.

Needless to say, like a good scientist, I again set about educating myself on the subject. I revisited my old friends on my library shelves. I asked the successful leaders who had become my friends and acquaintances over the previous two decades. Also, for the first time, I was able to look back over my own career as the leader of a great institution.

What I discovered was very different from—sometimes even counterintuitive to—many of the popular views of leadership. I began to see several crucial aspects of effective leadership: a strong foundation of principles, steadfastness to hold to those principles, and a set of methods to transform an institution and take it to a new level. The first four chapters of this book focus on the foundation: humility, authenticity, service, and empathy. Several of these have been associated with servant leadership,[1] but in my view these principles are critical to the kind of leadership that transforms an organization.

Chapter 5, "Courage," links these principles to methods for accomplishing an institutional transformation. Courage is both a characteristic of great leaders and a practice needed in challenging times.[2] Courage enables a leader both to stay the true course even when it is difficult and to abruptly alter course when necessary. Courage rests on the foundational principles of leadership as well as the core mission of an organization.

The final five chapters describe the methods I used to create transformational change—to take a great institution to new heights.

These chapters cover how we crafted a vision for the future of the university and engaged all members of the Stanford community in pursuing that vision. The chapters focus on collaboration, innovation, intellectual curiosity, storytelling, and creating change that lasts.

Transforming an institution more than one hundred years old requires a compelling vision, a determined team that executes to realize that vision, and steps to ensure that the transformation is long lasting. While the foundational leadership principles covered in the first four chapters were critical to developing and executing the ambitious plan we envisioned for Stanford, I relied on the leadership methods covered in the final five chapters to help us reach our goals.

Outside of Stanford, Phil Knight and I shared a deep concern over a growing leadership crisis in government, corporations, and nonprofits. From failed states to civil wars to famine to dictators made wealthy in poor developing countries to a rise in xenophobia and racism—the crises in government are obvious. In the corporate world, we see numerous examples of the leadership taking corporations astray, from old stories such as Enron and WorldCom to newer ones such as Wells Fargo and Volkswagen. The nonprofit world is not exempt from such crises either—just look at the way scandal-ridden athletics systems in colleges and universities stand in contrast to the lofty educational missions of these institutions.

Whether in government, commerce, or nonprofits, many of these issues arise because the leadership foundation is weak: leaders focus on their personal gains rather than the well-being of the organizations, employees, and customers they serve.

Harder to assess, but perhaps more prevalent, is the gap in understanding how to lead an organization through necessary transformations. Our world is changing at an ever-increasing pace. No matter how strong an organization's foundation or how long its history, all institutions must renew themselves if they are going to continue to thrive—and to serve—through the twenty-first century.

How do we right the course of leadership? I wrote this book partly to share my discoveries with you, and with the coming generations of Knight-Hennessy Scholars, including those who arrive after I am gone. First, though, I wrote this book for myself, to organize my own (sometimes painfully) acquired wisdom about leadership, and to take another look at key events in my career from a different, more removed perspective. Most of all, I wrote it to begin a conversation about the changing nature of leadership in the twenty-first century—a conversation that will, in some way, help inform the curriculum of the Knight-Hennessy Scholars program.

I offer this book to you, dear reader, from a man who started out with a very different dream but for whom the journey has been both challenging and immensely rewarding. May your journey have the same happy, if somewhat unpredictable, outcome.

1

HUMILITY

The Basis for Effective Leadership

"It is unwise to be too sure of one's own wisdom. It is healthy to be
reminded that the strongest might weaken and the wisest might err."
Mahatma Gandhi

Most people, looking from the outside, assume that *confidence* is the
heart of leadership. After all, if you aren't confident in your strategy and your role in it, it's almost impossible to lead others. No one
wants to follow a leader who seems unsure of his plans or her own
abilities. What lies at the heart of confidence?

I happen to think that real confidence—that is, not a mask of
confidence, or phony bravado, or worst of all, misplaced confidence,
but a true sense of one's own skills and character—arises not from
ego, but from humility. Arrogance sees only our strengths, ignores
our weaknesses, and overlooks the strengths of others, therefore leaving us vulnerable to catastrophic mistakes. Humility shows us where
our weaknesses lie so we can compensate for them. Humility makes
us earn our confidence.

Where does humility come from? In my experience, two perspectives encourage humility. First, we must realize that much of
our success is luck. I distinctly choose the word *luck* because the
alternative we might use, *fortune*, seems to imply some supernatural
intervention aligned with our interests. Face it, those of us born in
the United States are lucky. Think how different your opportuni-

ties would be if you were born in Haiti, the Congo, Bangladesh, or Afghanistan.

I grew up in a middle-class family, and both my parents had college educations. They taught me to read before I began school, and they provided career-enabling educational opportunities for me. Few of us in the United States, however, are very far from our more modest roots. Most of my ancestors immigrated during the Irish Potato Famine in the first half of the 1800s. My great-great-grandfather started as a hand laborer and later was a cart man, a person who made deliveries around Brooklyn with a hand or pony cart. In fact, all my great-great-grandparents did manual labor for their livings, from bricklayer to tanner to carpenter to farmer. Though they came from an English-speaking country, some of my Irish ancestors could not read or write, and their last wills and testaments are signed "X."

Two generations later, my maternal grandfather would attend college and eventually become a bank vice president. Those first- and second-generation immigrants lived tough lives, facing unemployment (often annually) and almost always suffering the death of at least one child (and sometimes two or more). I am the beneficiary of their hard work and their dedication to making a better life for their children and their children's children. My birth in this family, in this place, at this time—it was pure luck, built on the backs of my ancestors. Pondering such facts makes me feel humble.

Being a member of an academic community can also be humbling. There is always someone in the institution, and often in the same building, who knows more about almost any single subject than you do. (Indeed, it is likely there are students who know more about almost any single subject than you do.) This is a second perspective that encourages humility: you simply aren't the smartest person in the room. The success of the endeavor you are leading depends on the entire team. You need their expertise and assistance to succeed, so it's best to start by admitting what you don't know, learning what your team members do know, and humbly asking for their support.

Learning Humility Through Asking for Help

Fundraising is one of the best ways to practice humility while in a position of authority. When one is dealing with thousands of faculty members and staff, tens of thousands of students, and billions of dollars in budget and endowments, the power could go to one's head pretty quickly. The humble task of fundraising serves as an antidote.

If I include all the preparation that accompanies any successful fundraising effort, I estimate that I spent probably between one-third to one-half of my time raising money for the university. This was a big change for my family. For the first twenty-five years of our marriage, my wife had been accustomed to me coming home from teaching most days around 6 p.m. I didn't travel too frequently, since I was usually teaching. As president, suddenly I was attending events many evenings and flying off to meet with alumni nearly a dozen weekends per year, and even my daily lunches were mostly booked for some meeting or event—often in the name of fundraising.

Happily, I had lots of help. Typically, the hardworking alumni volunteers and Stanford's development professionals did most of the heavy lifting, nailing down thousands of smaller donations each year. Both groups are very good at what they do. I came to think of the university's development office as a matchmaker, finding and matching donors with important university needs, and I thought of the alumni association as caring for the long-term relationship between alumni and the university.

For my part, as university president, I understood I was merely a tool for these operations, not the engine itself. Be it a speech before a regional alumni group, a private meeting with a potential major donor, or an interview in the alumni magazine, my contribution came only at the end of a whole lot of preparatory work done by others. That too was a source of humility: I regularly reminded myself that I didn't make the deal. Many other people had worked on getting to "yes." I merely *closed* the deal. A mistake or wrong impression on my part could have ruined months of hard fieldwork. On top of that, I knew those alumni and major donors weren't meeting with me, John Hennessy the person, but with the president of Stanford University, a role that would someday be held by someone else.

That said, I recognized the importance of my role as the top representative of the university. Major donors wanted the handshake of the president, not because it's me, but because they wanted to know that the initiatives they had chosen to support would be backed by the university's attention and resources. They were asking me to put my reputation on the line beside their money. That was a big ask, and they had every right to make it.

As for the really big donations, those were almost always done one-to-one, often with no other staff in the room. It was just me and that famous, immensely successful, powerful individual who knew what he or she wanted, who was making a gigantic commitment, and who didn't hesitate to look me in the eye and ask if I was willing to make the same commitment. If that doesn't humble one, what will?

Humility at Work in the World

Jim Clark is one of the great entrepreneurs in high-tech history, but his early life was marked by great difficulty. His family was poor, he had a terrible stepfather, he dropped out of high school, and he joined the Navy because he saw no other future. Still, he proved to be a brilliant engineer—and a born entrepreneur. Jim first showed that talent when he founded Silicon Graphics, one of the fastest-growing companies of its era. Jim and I had shared an office suite at Stanford, and I had worked with him on a small part of the technology that became the basis for Silicon Graphics. I was also a consultant to Silicon Graphics for two years before I founded MIPS.

Frustrated at having to give away so much of the ownership of Silicon Graphics to venture capitalists, when Jim began building his next company, he did it by bootstrapping. Marc Andreessen (now one of the Valley's best-known VCs) was the lead creator of Mosaic, the first widely used visual browser. When the University of Illinois, where Marc was a student, decided to license the technology to a company that Marc was not involved in, Jim Clark swooped in, hired Marc, and began building a company that would market the first widely used, commercial Internet browser, Netscape. Largely forgotten now, Netscape was a brilliant play, thanks to Jim's perfect timing and insightful, strategic maneuvering. Jim had predicted the explosion in the use of the web, and he capitalized on it, creating the first World Wide Web company.

The success of Netscape, combined with his sizable equity in the company, made Jim Clark a very wealthy man. I had kept in touch with Jim over the years, and I knew how difficult his struggle to build those two companies had been. The man the world saw as an "overnight" billionaire I knew as a friend who had a number of personal issues. At one point Jim had been so focused on building the technology that would become Silicon Graphics, he had forgotten to pay his electricity bill, and the power had been turned off in his home. I had never seen anyone work harder; Jim had earned every penny of his fortune.

I thought a lot about Jim in those days. After all his success, I knew he was thinking about what to do with the rest of his life. Netscape was already his second act, so he could take some time to figure out his next step.

In 1999, under the leadership of my predecessor, President Gerhard Casper, Stanford had started a project called Bio-X, to build multidisciplinary collaborations focused on bioscience and bioengineering. As the dean of the School of Engineering, I was an enthusiastic supporter. We understood that making this new center successful would require significant philanthropic support, both for a facility and for research. Stem cell research was one particularly promising area, and it struck me that this activity might be something that would capture Jim's imagination. What better challenge for a great engineer than to help figure out how to use an emerging technology to solve difficult problems?

I had talked to Jim about doing something for Stanford after the success of Silicon Graphics, but he wasn't ready. Would he be ready after the success of Netscape? I knew I had to get Jim thinking a bit about his legacy; he had been working with his head down, so focused on immediate challenges that he had barely given himself enough time to think about the future. As it happened, I had just read *Titan*, the biography of John D. Rockefeller by Ron Chernow (who would later win a Pulitzer Prize for his biography of George Washington and write the biography of Hamilton that was the basis for the hit musical). As Chernow recounted, Rockefeller was a highly competitive entrepreneur who had made himself one of the wealthiest men in American history, but he nearly died in his fifties from a heart attack brought on by overwork.

It was an epiphany. Convinced that his time was short (in fact, he lived to be ninety-seven), Rockefeller decided, "I'm done with trying to make more money. I'm going to become a philanthropist and make the world a better place." Before long he had founded the University of Chicago, Rockefeller University, and the Rockefeller Foundation, and supported numerous other causes, particularly in medicine. In the process, he helped create modern philanthropy.

Rockefeller is most famous for giving dimes to children, but in fact he gave away billions for the improvement of humankind. One of the most infamous of the Robber Barons, and perhaps the most ruthless and competitive of that group, a humbled Rockefeller chose a very different trajectory for the second half of his life.

I sent Jim Clark a copy of the book. I hoped the story of one legendary workaholic would help another, a century later.

I let enough time pass for Jim to read the book, and then I contacted him and told him about the plans for our new interdisciplinary center and the work on stem cells and regenerative medicine. Jim spent a day visiting the campus and talking to the faculty researchers.

Jim is an intellectual and a scientist, and I hoped this interdisciplinary mix of engineering and the biosciences would excite him. It did, and that led to his commitment of $150 million to create the Clark Center, the home for Bio-X.

But that's not the end of the story.

Not long after Jim made his commitment, President George W. Bush announced that he was severely restricting federal government support of stem cell research. The news came as a shock, not just to those of us in the academic community, but to Jim Clark. He thought the decision was a disaster, one that really would hurt the research program he had just underwritten, and he felt he needed to make a statement. Ultimately, he announced to the world, via an editorial in the *New York Times*,

> Two years ago I pledged to donate $150 million to create a center for biomedical engineering and science at Stanford. Now Congress and the president are thwarting part of the intended purpose of this center by supporting restrictions on stem cell research and cloning. . . . I am therefore suspending $60 million of my remaining pledge.

We dedicated the building in 2003, with Jim in attendance and me in my role as university president. We continued to struggle to raise the $60 million we had lost with the suspension of Jim's pledge. Fortunately, the other major donor, Chuck Feeney, whose incredible thirty-year philanthropic legacy was made public only in 2012, remained steadfast. So we soldiered on, making the best of the situation, and seeing some real victories in our research. In 2004, in response to a brain drain of stem cell scientists to other countries, the State of California proposed and passed a bond issue to independently fund stem cell research. That staunched the loss of our most talented faculty members in the field, as well as other scientists around the state.

Roll forward to 2013, the tenth anniversary of the Clark Center. Over the intervening years, Jim had come by the university once or twice each year to check on the progress of the program. For the tenth anniversary, we decided to hold a big event, including an all-day seminar, to highlight the research breakthroughs and achievements of the decade. It was also a chance to say a big thank you to Jim and to show him that we had been good stewards of his gift. Jim was scheduled to be the last speaker.

When it came time for him to speak, I was sitting next to Jim. I had no clue what he was going to say. Would he revisit his past frustration? Would he attack the federal government for its short-sightedness? No one could have predicted what happened next.

Jim stood at the podium and said, "I'm so moved by what's been done here. This research is great. You guys have done a terrific job." He paused, and then added, "I'm sending you the remaining $60 million of my original pledge."

It was a stunning moment and a shining example of humility. Despite having made such a public pronouncement about retracting his donation, Jim Clark had reversed himself, because it was the right thing to do. I was hugely proud to be his friend.

Developing a Sense of Humility

Stepping up to the moment isn't something that came easily to me, or naturally. For the first half of my career, every talk I gave was accompanied by stacks of overhead projections or slides, usually filled with diagrams, text, and equations. Suddenly, as university president, I found myself talking to groups of every imaginable size—from that solitary major donor to twenty thousand guests at graduation—without a single overhead or slide, and occasionally without much time to prepare. Perhaps that comes easily for some people, but it certainly didn't for me. I had to learn step by step. Initially, at least, I found it terrifying.

Fortunately, though I certainly did not think it "fortunate" at the time, I had been dropped into the deep end earlier in my career. In 1986, I was thirty-four years old. We had founded MIPS Computer

Systems two years earlier, and it had enjoyed a fast start. In expectation of that kind of growth continuing, we staffed up just as fast with new employees. Unfortunately, that growth rate didn't continue. We were still expanding, revenues were still strong, and we were still cutting deals, but our expenses had shot up too quickly. We should have started raising money earlier, an activity precluded by a CEO transition. As a result, we were out of money and facing the possibility of missing the next month's payroll.

We had no choice but to do a layoff. Out of about 120 employees, we were going to have to let 40 of them go. The executive team decided that we would hold on to engineers, which made the hit fall harder on others. We gave out the pink slips on Friday morning, and those individuals were gone by noon.

It was awful, something I had never imagined we would have to experience, and something I never wanted to experience again. Such moments—if we are humble enough to receive them—give us the opportunity to learn from our mistakes and to change course, but that day wasn't done schooling me yet.

Next, our new CEO, Bob Miller, decided the best thing we could do was to hold an all-hands meeting for the "survivors" that afternoon. He asked me to get up and give a pep talk. I would have liked not to do it, but as a cofounder, I knew I needed to step up. I started by admitting that we had made mistakes, and then I tried to focus on the bright future that the company had ahead of it. In the end, I'm glad I gave that talk, because—though I didn't know it at the time—that talk, both admitting the mistakes and rallying the team, was the perfect preparation for my future.

Twelve years later, when my appointment as president of Stanford was announced, I had to get up in front of several hundred people and give a short speech describing my thoughts about my new position and the future of the university. It was, in fact, the first time I had *ever* given a formal speech in which I didn't have any audiovisual material as a crutch. I knew I could give a good technical talk or teach a class, but this was different, and I was nervous as hell. How did I get through it? Well, I felt humble about being chosen, so I focused on how honored I was, how much my predecessor had done for Stanford, and how I hoped I could help make Stanford a better university.

Those early experiences prepared me for situations that would arise throughout my professional life, including Stanford's reaction to 9/11 and the great recession of 2008, as we'll see in Chapter 5, "Courage."[1] Each of these events both humbled me and required me to rise to the challenge. In the end, they helped me grow as a leader.

Humility and Ambition

Before closing my thoughts on humility, I should add that when I speak of "humility," I'm not just describing a personality trait some people are born with, although reflecting on the good luck associated with your birth should contribute to your humility. Neither do I mean the sort of humility that focuses on self-deprivation. I mean an artful, directed humility—a practice you develop as a leader, like courage and decisiveness. Leading with humility means letting others announce your accomplishments because you don't need to, it means realizing and openly admitting that your understanding might not be right, it means willingly soliciting assistance because you know you need the help, it means taking the opportunity to learn from mistakes, and it means stepping up to the moments that challenge and grow you.

This kind of humility does not, however, mean a lack of ambition. Abraham Lincoln had a humble demeanor, but he was ambitious.[2] I, too, am ambitious, but my ambition is not focused primarily on personal gain (though I do like to win at games and golf). Instead, my ambition is to make a difference, to benefit the institution and the community I serve. Perhaps the only way to be both humble and ambitious is to be ambitious for the good of others.

Humility as a Basis for Personal Growth

Not long before I stepped down as president, I was reminiscing with one of the trustees who hired me, Isaac Stein, who also served as chair of the board during my presidency. Isaac was in the midst of leading the search for my successor. He said, "You know, John, in retrospect, the characteristic we got when we picked you as president was the ability to grow on the job."

I took that as a great compliment—and I tried not to cringe too much thinking about how green I had been when I had started fifteen years earlier. To Isaac, this ability to grow had proven more important than anything else, something he said he hadn't anticipated when I was hired. Now his committee was trying to calibrate that ability, to figure out how to measure it, so they could use it as a centerpiece in the search for my replacement.

How can someone gauge your ability to learn on the job? I suppose by assessing your humility. If you accept that you still have much to learn, that other people are better than you at certain things, and that the ideas of many are almost always better informed than the opinion of one, you can't help but be humble, and therefore dedicated to learning how to be better at what you do.

In a sense, when we put humility in the heart of leadership, the leader's role itself changes. I learned this at MIPS. In a start-up environment, where time is so compressed and even the littlest mistakes can be fatal, you have to lead not by separating yourself from your subordinates, but by becoming their equal on the team. Your job is not to tell people what to do, but to dedicate yourself to helping them do better. That's why at MIPS, when we were getting ready to send our first chip to the factory, and we had a shortage of folks to help with final verification, I jumped in to write a program to generate tests.

Our first CEO at MIPS, Vaemond Crane, operated similarly. He announced that we were going to have staff meetings on Saturday mornings, because he wanted to send a message to everyone in the company that they were expected to work at least a half day on the weekend. By calling those meetings, he made it clear that senior managers (including him) had to do their part too, but he sweetened this demand by showing up at those meetings with a box of donuts. This is the same CEO I saw wiping off the counters in the lunch-room, sending the message that he was no better than anyone else. In the stressful world of a hot new tech start-up, I deeply appreci-ated that gesture, and my memory of it has lingered all these years, informing my actions as a leader.

Though, like most people, I have a lot to be humble about, I'll be the first to admit that I'm not, by nature, a humble person. However, I have learned the importance of practicing humility. Perhaps the most important instances when you need to practice humility are when you have made the wrong decision. Mistakes happen to every leader, and it's better to accept them, to have the courage to admit the mistakes, and to decide how to move on. You will find several examples in this book where I needed to do just that. The process is not necessarily pleasant, but it is a lot easier if you are humble.

2

AUTHENTICITY
AND TRUST

The Essential Ingredients for Effective Leadership

"Be sure you put your feet in the right place. Then stand firm."
Abraham Lincoln

Maintaining one's integrity is often presented as the greatest challenge faced by adults in their professional and private lives. Perhaps. But I think there's an even greater challenge.

Please don't get me wrong. Living a life of integrity is no easy feat. Certainly, civilization could benefit from more of it. Many of my heroes—George Washington, Abraham Lincoln, Teddy Roosevelt, and David Packard—were considered the embodiment of integrity, trustworthiness, and honor. They were not perfect, no one is, but they got this characteristic mostly right.

When we talk about integrity, when we tell our children, "Don't lie, don't steal, don't cheat, and follow the rules, even when no one is looking," we are guiding them toward behaviors that tens of millions of people practice every day. With the help of everything from faith to family to fear of the law, integrity is eminently achievable and usually unambiguous.

Far more difficult to practice every day, especially as an adult, is *authenticity*, the practice of speaking honestly and being true not just to ourselves, but to others, to our communities, to the rest of humanity, even when being honest may subject us to criticism or lead to discord. Among the legions of people in the world who exhibit integrity in their dealings with others, how many are truly authentic?

Authenticity, a nuanced and multidimensional characteristic, is essential to building trust and therefore to successful leadership.[1] Most basically, we embody authenticity when we follow the advice Lincoln uttered to a nurse while helping her from a carriage: "Be sure to put your feet in the right place. Then stand firm." How do you decide where to stand? Once you decide, what does it take to hold the courage of your convictions?

Endeavor to Become

We can best understand the practice of authenticity first by understanding what it is not.

A child of the 1960s, I experienced the precursor to today's popular authenticity movement. Breaking away from prescribed social roles and expectations, a generation of young adults began experimenting with what it meant to be "real," meaning true to one's atavistic impulses, free of external laws and rules. I understand that philosophy, but as someone who has lived through the subsequent half century, I have also witnessed the calamities unleashed by its full-throated adoption. Equally alarming is an authenticity that values "winning" by any means or at all costs. We are human beings, not mere animals. To my mind, our greatest task is to learn how to improve ourselves, to become all that we can be.

More recently, we are seeing the rise of the "authentic leadership" movement. The name, at least, appears to have originated at the Harvard Business School, and has spread through the management press and the messages of popular business speakers, becoming less and less precise as it goes.

I'm wary of business theories that explode in popularity and suddenly seem to be on everybody's lips. Some disappear just as quickly. In its diluted form, "authentic leadership" amounts to buzzword advice, like "lead with honesty, humility, a sense of humor, openness, and candor." Undoubtedly these are positive leadership traits, but the authenticity I'm talking about requires more.

Consider the wisdom popularly attributed to Socrates: "The way to a good reputation is to endeavor to be what you desire to appear." It's a start down the path to a deeper practice of authenticity—you must identify those good and true characteristics you admire, and then you must work to embody them.

Our predecessors understood what we have largely forgotten: that as much as we are constrained by nature, with dedication and practice we can become what we choose to be. Perhaps no greater example is found in American history than George Washington. His ambition to leave a legacy drove his self-discipline and personal development. He assiduously copied down and practiced rules of behavior to become a man of honor, bravery, and virtue. He didn't start out that way; even in his twenties he was still torn by impetuousness. By the time he commanded the Continental Army, and certainly as president of the United States, that figure he aspired to be had become his authentic self—a fact recognized by both friend and foe.

So this is part of the practice: identify the virtues you admire, strive to embody them, and be humble about the journey—you probably aren't there yet. In fact, just when you think you've arrived, life has a way of returning you back to the beginning.[2]

In my journey, the difficult decisions concerned two questions: what path to follow in my career and what position to take on issues that split the community I was leading. Once I had decided where to place my feet, the challenge came in standing firm, usually by articulating the rationale that brought me to the place I chose to stand.

Being Authentic and Truthful Can Be Difficult

Speaking the truth is easy when we stand on the side of the majority, when we see few consequences and sure rewards. In such cases, being lauded as a truth-teller feels good. However, speaking the difficult truth—whether sharing unfortunate news or risking rejection, humiliation, bodily injury, or large-scale social ostracism—feels a whole lot different. We like to think that we would stand up against wrongdoing at great personal risk, or we would leave a fortune on the table out of honor, or we would choose to be shunned by society before we would contradict our principles, but would we? Practicing authenticity at this level proves a lot more difficult than merely fulfilling the basic tenets of integrity.

Even if we're acting for the greater good, sharing a difficult truth can be painful, especially when the truth will hurt people we care about. It's not surprising then that many people avoid at all costs this opportunity to practice authenticity. It may surprise you, however, to learn that even some of the best-known powerful leaders, in Silicon Valley and beyond, find truth-telling extremely difficult. Steve Jobs is perhaps the one person I've met who didn't care much about being liked by his colleagues and therefore could be brutally honest. For most of us, however, being liked is an important part of our social well-being.

Few of us want to be the kind of person who hurts others' careers, disrupts lives, or disappoints ambitious employees. However, when we avoid, for example, firing a disruptive employee or conducting a necessary layoff, we inadvertently create bigger problems, potentially interfering with the functionality or morale of a team, or the sustainability of the organization.

Ironically, some business leaders, unwilling to bear the emotional weight of firing an employee or doing a layoff, sometimes hire a "hatchet man," often in the form of a consultant, to do the dirty work for them. This move bypasses what can be a learning opportunity. While it may provide temporary relief, in the end the message to the rest of the company is transparent: this leader is afraid to step up to the job when the job gets tough.

Other executives may struggle to be truthful about business matters. Some CEOs just can't say no. They want to be the good boss, the encouraging boss, the one who signs on to every new proposal placed on his or her desk. What happens when saying yes to one employee's dreams results in negative consequences for the whole company? You have also probably witnessed indecisive bosses—those who switch opinions depending on the last person with whom he or she spoke. Employees see through this, quickly learning to be the last person to talk to the boss.

While giving the people-pleasing answer might feel good in the moment, the consequences will haunt the organization for a long time. Better to follow the path of authenticity: understand the overall mission and direction—*put your feet in the right place*—and make the tough calls—*stand firm*.

Why Authenticity Is Critical in Leadership

Early in my career as a college administrator, I found myself in the uncomfortable position of needing to tell a colleague that if they didn't make some important changes, they were not going to get tenure. Making matters worse, I had helped hire this person, who had been a superstar job candidate. On the job, this professor had lots of potential, but also some significant shortcomings.

Though it would not be an easy message to deliver, I knew I had to do it. If I didn't encourage change, both the institution and the individual would suffer; both would be less than they could be. I knew I would be doing my colleague a tremendous disservice if I held back. So I delivered the message. I'm embarrassed to admit that I didn't do it as promptly or as articulately as I could have, which was a mistake, but I did it eventually.

Over the years, I've always tried to deliver bad news instead of hiding from it or passing that responsibility to others. Certainly I have never enjoyed the process. Nor did I always do it as promptly as I could have, nor without sleepless nights. It's a struggle to balance your empathy and humane tendencies against the requirements of your job: to be authentic and honest. These are the moments that invite you to live up to the authentic ideals you have chosen for yourself—to act as the leader you strive to be, even when the person you currently are feels uncomfortable. These experiences are how we grow into the leaders we aspire to be, one uncomfortable moment at a time.

Running a large institution puts one in contact with many different communities and circumstances over the course of even a single day, and each constituency has unique expectations. As a result, during my presidency I found myself drawing on various facets of myself—my actual characteristics, my desired characteristics, my personal history, my professional experiences—from one moment to the next. One could say a leader needs to be many different "selves" throughout a day, but if one wants to be perceived by his or her various constituents as consistent, truthful, and trustworthy—in other words, as authentic—then each of those "selves" must ultimately be one's own.

Why is it so important to make these authentic connections? Because there will come a time when you will need to ask all of these people to follow you in a particular direction, one that may not be an ideal fit for their own ambitions or plans but that clearly leads the institution to the greater good. If they don't trust you, if they don't believe that you have their welfare and that of the larger community at heart, they will not get behind you.[3] Putting yourself in that position in the corporate world is bad enough. In the case of a university, imagine what it is like to deal with many constituencies (faculty, staff, students, trustees, and alumni) who often hold differing views, and one of whom (tenured professors) enjoys perfect job security. If a university president has not gained the trust of all of those constituencies, his or her career will be ineffective and likely short.

I don't have to tell you that building this trust is not something that happens overnight. My view has always been that leading any complex institution is a marathon, not a sprint. You need to think in the long term. Short-term thinking, such as putting off the termination of an employee or continuing an initiative that isn't gaining traction, will undermine your effectiveness as a leader. Ultimately, you build trust with your constituents when you face up to tough decisions, something I'll talk more about in Chapter 5, "Courage."[4]

Building Trust with Other Constituents

Certainly, authenticity is critical to building trust with the employees in a company or a university, but it is also critical in dealing with other constituencies. Although corporations and universities are very different, they both have an internal constituency (employees) and a set of "external" constituencies that are approximate parallels of one another (Figure 1).

How did trust grow in my relationships with these constituencies? With the board of trustees, I resolved to give the "true scoop" on any situations that arose. Further, they came to understand that my support for a proposed decision was based on my view that it was in the best interests of Stanford. On the flip side, I had to trust that the board would stick by me: once a decision was made, we were unified. This unity did not necessarily mean unanimous agreement, but it did mean that once we decided to greenlight an initiative, the board backed the leadership 100 percent, even when the circumstances shifted slightly and we adjusted course. Note that committing to a course did not mean that no one had any doubts; there are always uncertainties. For a major new initiative to be successful, however, the leadership and board had to be fully committed at the start. (For example, see Chapter 5, "Courage," for the story of our aborted mission to establish a Stanford campus in New York.) This trusting relationship enabled the university leadership and the board to act collaboratively, thus allowing us to share our ideas and vision before they were fully shaped. This capability was crucial to developing the strategic plan that became the Stanford Challenge (for the full story,

FIGURE 1

Corporation	*University*
Board of Directors	Board of Trustees
Customers	Students/Parents and Research Funders
Shareholders	Alumni and Donors

see Chapter 7, "Innovation"), as well as formulating the vision for the Knight-Hennessy Scholars.

As a corporate board member, I have operated in the same manner. I expect the company leadership to be honest and forthcoming. Although the board may ask tough questions and challenge the leadership, once a decision is made, the board and leadership team are joined. I'll return to building a strong working relationship with the board in Chapter 6, "Collaboration and Teamwork."

With students and parents, I attempted to develop a trust relationship by being available, open to questions, and candid in my responses. Each year, as prospective students and their families considered Stanford during Admit Weekend, I would meet with them, and during Parents' Weekend, I would meet with parents of active students. In both cases, after a short opening speech, I opened an extended Q&A session. Parents asked about everything from bike helmets to teaching ethics, from financial aid to finding an advisor. I would do my best to answer them accurately and honestly. For example, frequently parents would ask why we didn't ban alcohol in all campus dorms and police the ban vigorously. I responded that such an approach would create undesired effects: students would drive off-campus to consume alcohol, which was clearly more dangerous, or they would drink covertly, increasing the risk that a highly intoxicated student might not get help. Instead, I explained, understanding that students would find a way to drink no matter what, we focused on getting them to watch out for each other and to call for help if anyone needed it.

During much of my presidency, I made it a practice to try to visit as many of the freshmen residences as I could, usually getting to almost all the residences with a majority of freshmen. In these meetings, I would briefly describe my history at Stanford and then open the floor for questions. The students' inquiries ran the gamut: from boxers or briefs to favorite places on campus to great courses to choosing a major to tough issues such as immigration reform, the Iraq war, or California's three strikes law.

The students advocating for divestment of the endowment from assets of fossil fuel companies were among the most passionate. In answer to their questions, I explained that the trustees had a process for considering divestment, which included a test of whether the company was causing social injury. Of course, in the case of fossil fuels, the hard problem is balancing the social benefits from energy against the harm from climate change. We did not divest from all fossil fuels, but we did make the decision to divest from companies involved in mining and using thermal coal (coal that is burned for energy purposes). While it was impractical for the United States (and the university) to abandon all fossil fuels, it was possible to eliminate coal and replace it with less damaging alternatives, such as natural gas. Though the decision to eliminate only coal did not satisfy many of the students, we could have a civil discussion about it. I could authentically say I believed it was the right answer, even though the broader divestment had some merits.

The goal of my visits to the freshmen residences was to begin to develop a relationship with the students. I wanted them to get to know me as a person, to understand that I was striving to do what I thought was in the best interests of the entire university, and to demonstrate that I believed that rational decision making was the modus operandi. I hoped those insights would form the basis of a trust relationship going forward, and they usually did.

Just as it was crucial that I be open and trustworthy with students and their families, corporations must develop trust relationships with their customers. Corporations that mislead their customers about product capabilities, availability, or reliability will lose those customers and damage their reputations, making it harder to recover by replacing the lost customers. The recent spate of corporate scandals, which clearly involved deceiving customers, is a reminder that once trust is lost, it is hard to regain.

The importance of trust is one of the reasons why Google works so hard to keep its search results authentic and unbiased and why the site separates search results from ads. If users do not believe in the validity of Google's search algorithms, they will abandon the use of Google.

As a corporate board member, I also came to understand the importance of trust between a corporation and its shareholders. This type of trust goes beyond the more minimal standard of honesty demanded by the Sarbanes-Oxley Act. Do the shareholders believe that the management team is honestly assessing its challenges and opportunities? If not, why should they hold the company's equity versus that of another?

A university's relationship with alumni and donors is even more crucial than the relationship between a corporation and its shareholders. After all, the shareholders can be replaced, although doing so may be painful and require a discount on the current stock value. In contrast, alumni and donors are built up over decades and cannot be replaced.

To engage this constituency, to share what was happening at the university, and to discuss our vision for the future of Stanford, we hosted events at which I would share my deep enthusiasm for the institution I was leading and the opportunities we had. This excitement was crucial to inspiring alumni and donors to support our work and our mission, and it worked because it was authentic. My enthusiasm, my drive to lead—these were born from my deep commitment to and belief in the institution, and my desire to see our plans come to fruition.

Beyond inspiration, a potential donor must share a trust relationship with the university, just as a customer considering a major purchase must trust the supplier. A major donor working with the president on a significant gift must trust that the president and the institution are fully committed to the goals of the gift. In many cases, the president is confirming the institutional importance of a potential gift, often with resources that are needed in addition to the gift by the donor. This trusted relationship leads to new initiatives that would not exist without substantial donor commitment.

Authentic Leadership: A Journey of Growth and Understanding

I was lucky to have found my interest in computing while still in high school, and early in my college years, I decided I wanted to be a professor. I've never deviated from that path, or regretted it. Even when I took an 80 percent leave from Stanford to help found the fabless semiconductor company MIPS, I always believed I would return to the university. For forty years, Stanford University has been my long-term, full-time employer, the only one I've ever had. I suppose that makes me an anomaly in Silicon Valley, where having three or more employers over the course of two decades is much closer to the norm.

Is sticking with one employer over one's entire career more conducive to developing a reputation for principled authenticity? Perhaps. Certainly the prospect of being loyal to a single employer for decades—and dealing with the same colleagues for an equal amount of time—reinforces that behavior. In a few cases, however, the academic life can lead to a kind of decadence and a jaded attitude. If you can't be fired, why go the extra mile, push yourself harder, take on new challenges, and make the tough decisions? Simple: because your reputation is your most valuable asset. Standing still will not enhance it, but will slowly erode it.

By comparison, a fast-moving corporate career opens one up to temptations: to cut corners, to reach for the short-term gain, to undermine one's peers. After all, if things go awry, one can switch companies and start over. That said, the constant change of environment and the need to compete for every rung up the latter also reinforces normative behavior. That's why some of the most enlightened, honest, and honorable—the most authentic—people I know are corporate CEOs. A person may be able to get near the top by being ruthless, but few boards of directors, and even fewer shareholders, will let a destructive person anywhere near the levers of power.

Let's go back to the beginning. You don't have to know, when you are young, who you want to be. In my experience, very few young adults have set life goals, or at least not the goals they will eventually live out. Much of your career path is about knowing where you're headed today, but not necessarily knowing the final destination. It's not fixed yet. You're creating that destination—and yourself—as you go. Some core values may be built in you when you're really young, but so much more develops over time, from your own life experiences, watching other people, or reading great biographies. It's always less painful to learn from others when you can. (Again, see the Coda for an annotated list of some of my favorite biographies.)

Similarly, few leaders are fully formulated when they start their leadership journey. Lincoln's position on slavery is a good example: early on he was personally opposed, but not an abolitionist. He later became adamantly opposed to the growth of slavery, believing it immoral, and he issued the Emancipation Proclamation, under the guise of wartime necessity. Finally, only months before his assassination, he shepherded the Thirteenth Amendment through ratification, rendering slavery unconstitutional. Over time, he became a more authentic champion for "all men are created equal."[5]

For me, leadership has been a journey involving different roles with enlarging responsibility. My love for both teaching and research led me to an academic career. I could happily have spent my entire life engaged in the rewarding and fulfilling role of professor. I never set out to be, nor wanted to be, either the founder of a start-up or a university president. My understanding that I could take on those roles, authentically and enthusiastically, came over time.

In the early 1980s, a group of faculty and students at Stanford had started a research project on how to design microprocessors, and we discovered insights similar to those found by parallel projects at IBM and Berkeley, all of which led to the Reduced Instruction Set Computer (RISC) revolution. We published our papers and assumed that our colleagues in industry would build on the advances we had discovered, which were obviously superior to the existing approaches. That did not happen.

Then, Gordon Bell, one of the early employees of DEC (then the second-largest computer company after IBM) came to see me. He recognized the advantages of the technology we had discovered, and he argued that if we really wanted to see this innovation thrive, we needed personally to commit to it by starting a company based on those discoveries. Otherwise, he said, our papers would sit on the shelf, ignored. He was asking me to answer two questions: Do you really believe your research results are as transformative as you have claimed? If so, are you willing to commit to developing the technology, taking the risk that it might not work out?

Though the decision-making process felt a bit torturous—it's not easy to alter one's set course—in the end, I answered yes. Of course, I had some doubts, and in retrospect, had I understood how little I knew about starting a company, I might have answered differently. Nonetheless, with the help of my two cofounders, MIPS was born and became influential in establishing the RISC approach. The core concepts remain at work today, some thirty-plus years later. In fact, just as I am doing the final edits, Dave Patterson (the leader of the Berkeley RISC project) and I received the Turing Award (the highest award in computer science) for the discoveries we made.

My journey to university leadership emerged out of my growing understanding of the role of leadership as service and my deepening, authentic loyalty to Stanford and its core mission. The real change in course happened when I was invited to move from dean of the School of Engineering to provost of the university.

In my role as dean, I had managed to keep alive the thread of teaching and research—the passions that drove me to academia. I was still advising a few PhD students, attending some major conferences, continuing to revise both textbooks I had coauthored, and teaching a course every year or two. Although my primary task was leading the engineering school, I had maintained an ongoing, if smaller, role as a teacher and scholar.

Then, one Friday afternoon, President Gerhard Casper asked me if I would be interested in serving as provost. A provost might teach on rare occasions, or give a few guest lectures, but essentially it's a full-time leadership role. As provost, I did not see how I could continue to work with PhD students, especially in a fast-moving field like information technology. How would I feel about giving that up? Could I really do the job well? I asked for the weekend to think about it.

That weekend, the outgoing provost, Condoleezza Rice, was giving a talk at the Founder's Day celebration, our annual celebration honoring the Stanfords' founding of the university. I still vividly remember her speech, some eighteen years later. Condi talked about her grandfather, a poor but hardworking black sharecropper in Alabama. She related how he had discovered that he could go to college, if he chose to study to become a Presbyterian minister.[6] She described how her grandfather's opportunity had transformed the Rice family and its trajectory. It enabled his son to go to college, and his granddaughter, Condi, to earn a spot on the Stanford faculty and eventually to serve as U.S. Secretary of State. In conclusion, she expressed her deep commitment to education, saying she had taken the role of provost because she believed in the power of education to transform lives, as it had for the Rice family.

In that moment, I knew the question I had to ask myself: Did I feel deeply committed to the mission of the university? Not just my own research or teaching, or just the engineering school, but did I believe that the entire university—from medicine to the humanities and social sciences to law and education and business—was engaged in critical work? Did I feel I could authentically commit to lead the entire institution with passion?

After hearing Condi's speech, I knew the answer. On Monday morning I told President Casper I would be his new provost. I had come upon my Rubicon. After reflection and some inspiration from Condi, I crossed it.

3

LEADERSHIP AS SERVICE

Understanding Who Works for Whom

"It is better to lead from behind and to put others in front, especially
when you celebrate victory when nice things occur. You take the front
line when there is danger. Then people will appreciate your leadership."
Nelson Mandela

For many people I know in positions of power and authority the
hardest thing to learn—and some never do learn it—is that *leadership
is service*.

It is a difficult lesson because almost every other aspect of being
a leader convinces leaders otherwise: leaders typically are paid more
money than most of the people they lead, leaders hold authority
over their teams, their decisions take priority, and their subordinates
are ultimately dedicated to serving *their leader* (or more precisely, the
institutions they lead).

In the face of all that, it can be hard to remember that *you*, the
leader, are serving *them*—they are doing the heavy lifting, while your
job is to help make them as effective and productive as they can be.[1]
To think this way, you have to mentally invert the organization chart,
so that the apex of the pyramid, where you sit, is at the bottom, supporting the rest. The truth is—and experience has only convinced
me even more deeply of this fact—if you can't accept, and live, your
role as a servant-leader, you will not be able to lead the institution
well. You will focus too much on your own gains and not enough on

the community and institution you are leading. In the long term, you will fail as the leader.

When I was thinking about becoming dean of Stanford's School of Engineering, I received the most influential piece of leadership advice from Jim Gibbons, the person I would be replacing. He told me, "Don't take this job because you like the title or you like the accouterments that come with the job. Take it because you want to serve your faculty colleagues and the students. Because that's really what the job is all about."

I thought a lot about this insight, and ultimately I decided, "Okay, yeah. I am willing to do that." I've tried to follow Jim Gibbons's advice ever since. In fact, it was the central part of my decision-making process when I was contemplating whether or not to leave the dean's job or the provost's. In saying yes and stepping up, I learned something interesting: the larger one's leadership role becomes, the bigger the role of service in that leadership.

I had started out leading a small research group. There, my job basically was helping graduate students successfully complete their research. When I was named head of a research laboratory, I was helping to hire, mentor, and develop younger faculty members. I may have held the leadership title and carried a degree of responsibility, but it was the work of those students and professors that mattered. I served the endeavor of their success. When I became chair of the computer science department, my primary goal remained the same: help the faculty and students succeed. As dean of the engineering school, I strove to serve on a much larger scale—to make sure the school ran well. Did its success or failure affect my reputation? Of course, but I couldn't create that success myself. Rather, my own success hinged on helping every other member of the school succeed. My career largely existed in reflection of theirs.

When I became the university president, the same role mapped out over a much wider landscape of constituents. Now the people I served included the students, faculty, staff, and alumni of the whole school. My "family" had expanded from a few people in the lab depending upon me to tens of thousands of people, scattered across hundreds of buildings, engaged in work in more than one hundred different units. Yet the task remained essentially the same: to lead the institution on a journey of success, by serving each of those constituencies in a manner that maximized the likelihood of our collective success.

That, I believe, was the real message from my predecessor as dean: if you take a leadership role as a step toward a personal goal of gathering ever-greater titles, awards, and salaries, you will never see true success in that role. The load of leading will only get bigger and heavier with each step, until you find yourself unable to advance it alone. In contrast, if you define your task as enlisting everybody to help push your institution in a direction you have devised with their support, you will all arrive at your destination, together.

Remember: *humility*. It is not enough to understand how many people are depending upon you; it is just as important to realize how much you are depending upon them. Every person who works for you has an important role to play in the day-to-day operations of the institution. That's why I thank the custodian when he comes in while I am working late. I may sign his paycheck, but he keeps the workspace clean and usable.

Whom Do You Serve? Taking the Long-Term View

If leadership is about service, whom does a leader serve? As mentioned in the last chapter, universities and corporations have a parallel set of stakeholders: employees, customers, and shareholders in the case of corporations; employees (faculty and staff), students (and their families), and alumni in the case of universities. In both cases, the leadership must balance the needs and desires of these groups. In doing so, a question arises: Should a leader address the short-term or long-term needs?

In the corporate world, that answer is complex. Even within one group, such as shareholders, people hold different viewpoints, with some focusing on short-term returns while others look for long-term investments. Customers may split similarly, between potential repeat customers who favor a long-term perspective and buyers looking for the best one-time transaction. Employees, especially those who have formed a loyal commitment to the company, are likely to hold a long-term perspective. In my view, part of the job of a leader in the corporate world is to balance these long-term and short-term interests. Often leaders face pressure to focus on quarterly earnings and short-term returns, and if a leader expects to have a short tenure, he may well favor those short-term interests. The leader who expects to have a long-term tenure, however, should have her interests (and her compensation) aligned with the long-term success of the organization and its stakeholders.

In a university, this long-term focus comes somewhat more naturally. The university analogue of a corporation's stock price is its reputation, and all its stakeholders have an interest in that reputation. Certainly blunders, such as a financial or academic scandal, can affect the reputation of the university in the short term. By and large, however, the university's reputation is tied to long-term factors, and this relationship encourages appropriate long-term thinking. The challenge in a university is that the diversity of the stakeholders could lead to differing views on priorities and directions. Balancing those in the long-term best interests of all is the challenge.

What does a long-term focus mean? In my mind, it means thinking five to ten years out for a corporation and ten to twenty for a university. Of course, that does not mean one can ignore the short-term issues, but it does mean thinking about new directions and developments that will ensure a healthy trajectory for the organization in the future. In both my academic and my high-technology corporate experience, this long-term view is also critical because new discoveries and inventions happen frequently and can often change the landscape of challenges and opportunities. Keeping the institution in a top position requires constantly exploring future opportunities and ensuring the team is poised to pursue an emerging new direction. This longer-term perspective is necessary for fostering new directions and opportunities, as I discuss in Chapter 7, "Innovation."

Sometimes, an even longer-term perspective can be helpful in setting goals. When I was preparing the speech for my inauguration in October 2000, I started thinking about the individuals who had led Stanford in the 109 years since its founding. I focused on the first president, David Starr Jordan, and on the many goals that he and the Stanfords had gotten right when establishing and leading the university. I hearkened back to words from Jordan's inauguration speech: "*It is for us as teachers and students in the university's first year to lay the foundations of a school which may last as long as human civilization.*" That long-term focus led me to ask four questions: What does Stanford stand for? What shall we be in ten years? In one hundred years? How do we ensure that future generations of our community will have the same opportunities that we have had? That last question shaped my thinking when I faced the really big challenges, whether crises or opportunities. Of course, thinking long-term introduces more uncertainty and can raise doubts about a direction, including in the mind of the leader. The price of avoiding those doubts, however, is to choose a path that is more short-term and incremental, which was certainly not my style.

Of course, leadership as service does not end at the boundaries of an organization's campus. In addition to serving the short-term and long-term goals of Stanford's direct stakeholders, I looked to the broader community in which Stanford existed, acknowledging the implicit obligations we had to that community. For leaders, the calls to serve our communities come in two forms: those that are directed at the leaders and those that engage a larger portion of the organization. Let's consider them in that order.

The Leader in Service to the Community

One of the realities of leadership is that the higher one climbs in terms of responsibility, the more the world will ask one to serve outside one's core constituencies. A person elected president or named CEO of an institution or enterprise of any size likely will be asked to sit on boards of directors, government committees, blue ribbon panels, and other forms of high-profile advisory groups. Even in lower-level leadership positions, she or he may be asked to serve on a community foundation, or to advise local government, or to join the board of a local nonprofit. For leaders committed to service, it is very hard to say no to these invitations, especially when they come with cries for help, or from organizations that assist the disadvantaged, or with a call to serve the national interest.

How do you decide which invitations to accept and which to decline?

Regretfully, you must learn to say no to most of these requests. Why? For one, it would be physically impossible to do them all. In addition, if you overextend yourself, the constant mental multitasking will diminish your capacity to engage in the long-term thinking required by your own institution. I have watched leaders become so involved in their volunteer work, often in Washington or its orbits, that their own organizations suffer. That's a mistake. Ultimately, any external service you render must be tempered by the fact that your first duty is to your organization and its stakeholders.

This is not to diminish the work of government advisory groups or nonprofits. On the contrary, putting together the best advisory boards they can is part of what governments and nonprofits need to do to thrive. As someone who assembled more than his share of boards and committees of volunteers at Stanford, I know how important and influential such roles can be.

Nevertheless, there must be a limit to this kind of service. In the early part of a leader's career, volunteer opportunities often provide interesting learning environments, which can complement other experiences—those invitations are worth considering. As I progressed in my career, I used a three-part filter:

How important was the service and the institution being served?
Could I contribute in an impactful way or could others easily provide the service?
Would the service opportunity contribute to my learning and growth?

No matter where you are in your career, before making a commitment, consider the following: in good times, you may readily say yes to an invitation that you later regret in times when your primary constituents require more from you. Further, in declining invitations, I often said, "I can't do it this year," which left the door open for a further request, "How about next year or the year after?" This response leads to a new problem: you can't predict your availability that far in advance. If you say yes, when the time arrives you may regret the commitment. Fulfilling that commitment could put your ability to serve your own institution at risk, but breaking the commitment would put your personal integrity on the line. Instead, upon the initial invitation, look ahead to the following month. Ask yourself, "Would I still want to do this then?" If your answer is yes, this is an opportunity to explore. If your answer is no, better to say that difficult no now—to be authentic—than to find yourself in a conundrum later down the line.

Service by the Institution as Part of the Mission

Personal service is only part of the role of the servant-leader. Leaders of corporations, nonprofits, government agencies, and universities also support a variety of external service initiatives for their organizations, beginning with service to the broader world that occurs as a natural consequence of the pursuit of their institutions' core missions.[2]

For example, corporations serve their customers by providing a useful product, often even a product that changes lives for the better.

Beyond that, they may choose to provide service that is an extension of their product offerings, often an extension that has social value, rather than a profit motive. In addition, corporations may be called upon to perform more general community service, for example, to aid the people who live where they work.

As might be expected due to their mission and status, nonprofits are more frequently called upon than corporations to engage in public service. Likewise, government agencies, because they serve the people, are often called upon.

Universities, in advancing the frontiers of knowledge, make discoveries and create inventions that can be put to work to enhance the quality of life and better functioning of society. Similarly, by educating students, the university serves the needs of both students and future employers. Further, universities create initiatives to connect their resources with the needs of their surrounding communities.

The notion of the university as a public service is deeply embedded in Stanford's history. Most people in the world don't know that what we call "Stanford University" is actually named Leland Stanford Jr. University. It is not named after the famous railroad man, governor, and senator, but rather after his son, who died just before he was sixteen. Both Leland Sr. and his wife Jane were so shattered by the loss of their only child that they resolved to build a university in their son's name, with the aim that henceforth "the children of California shall be our children."

Jane had prepared a speech for the first opening day in 1891, just as I did during the sixteen years I served as president. On that day in 1891, she was ultimately too emotional to deliver it. In that speech she wrote,

> I hope that your lives will be truly earnest, not in the sense of going forth to acquire great wealth and great names; but to be conscientious workers, to be helpful to others, to send cheer and goodwill to those that need lifting up, and to always follow the Golden Rule.

Leland Stanford Sr. died less than two years later, and the university was thrown into financial turmoil. Jane steered the university through more than ten difficult years, at significant personal sacrifice. In 1904, she stepped down as trustee, turning the university over to its first independent board, with the following words:

> Through all these years I have kept a mental picture before me. I could see a hundred years ahead when all the present trials were forgotten, and all of the present active parties gone, and nothing remaining but the institution. I could see beyond all this the children's children's children coming here from the East, the West, the North, and the South.

I have taken that last sentence to heart, as have all of my predecessors and my successor. While we have a founding document and deed of trust, these personal statements about the goals of the university and the founder's wishes that the university "promote the public welfare by exercising an influence in behalf of humanity and civilization," have cemented the notion of the university as public service in our psyches. That notion makes the president's responsibility clear: his or her leadership serves an organization that serves the greater good.

Whether one leads in a university, corporation, nonprofit, or government agency, the questions remain the same: How should leaders think about the role of public service? How should leaders choose which initiatives to support? The service initiatives that Stanford launched or expanded during my tenure as president have informed my answers to these questions. In particular, three community initiatives that Stanford undertook in our nearby communities—the Stanford Charter School, the Community Law Clinic, and the Cardinal Free Clinics—all aimed to provide service to the less privileged inhabitants of our area.

Colleagues in the School of Education began the Stanford Charter School project in the 1990s and opened the school in my first year as president. East Palo Alto, an economically depressed area, had lost its only public high school twenty-five years earlier, as part of desegregation efforts. Many of the lower-income students from the neighborhood were struggling at the two district high schools; their graduation rates were disappointing and college attendance was rare. The goal of Stanford Charter School was to create an educational environment informed by the latest thinking from the university, where students would receive critical advising and support services. It worked: graduation rates went up by almost one-third, and college attendance rates more than doubled. Later in my tenure, the goal became to expand the school, adding lower grades to eventually create a complete K–12 school.

While some doubts were raised about the university's ability to expand and operate the larger school, there was real enthusiasm among some faculty in our education school and the Stanford philanthropic community. After assessing the concerns, we decided to proceed. Once the school was opened, the children and their families loved it—the students benefitted from committed young teachers, as well as extensive after-school and advising programs. Visiting the school was a moving experience: hearing students—who had been performing far below grade-level when they had started at the school, whose families were often struggling to get by—speak with pride about their education and their college goals.

The project, however, encountered a big problem. A school is not merely a research project or a hobby; it is a real business, and a complicated one at that. Operating a school requires expertise in hiring principals and teachers, managing finances, and maintaining infrastructure. These skills fell outside of the expertise of my colleagues who had launched the program, and no one wanted to sacrifice completely his or her research and teaching career to run the school, especially given their limited experience in the more practical areas of running the "business." The challenges of running the larger school, initially raised by some members of the team, had come true.

Ultimately, Stanford turned the facility over to a professional charter school operator. The pedagogical innovations and advising services that led to founding the school were a natural extension of the School of Education's mission, but the rigors of running the school were not. Stanford's Graduate School of Education continues to provide guidance on issues such as innovations in pedagogy—service that is an extension of its mission—while others handle the day-to-day school operations.

By comparison, the Community Law Clinic in East Palo Alto has proven sustainable as an extension of the mission of the law school. The clinic provides free legal advice and representation for people in the community, as well as offering valuable experience for law school students. Like all of our legal clinics, this one is overseen by a faculty member and staffed by law school students, with minimal administrative support and some core financial backing from the law school.

On the other hand, Cardinal Free Clinics, which operates free medical clinics in both Menlo Park and San Jose, falls between these two models. Its main staffing is provided by volunteer physicians and student volunteers, primarily medical students, but the clinics also employ staff for nursing and administration. This program relies on financial support both from the School of Medicine, from the hospitals and from donors, but its financial and staffing needs are much smaller than those of the charter school; therefore it remains in that sweet spot of providing service while extending—and not detracting from—the School of Medicine's core mission.

All three of these activities started as experiments. Two have worked well and appear to have ongoing vitality, but that isn't always the case with service initiatives. The more an initiative veers from an institution's core mission, the less likely it is to achieve long-term success. If an initiative isn't working, best to face up to it and seek a viable exit strategy that minimizes the harm to the community being served. Fortunately, we found an alternative that allowed the charter school to thrive.

No matter what kind of organization you lead, with creativity and commitment, your organization can come up with initiatives that both extend your core mission and serve the communities closest to you.

Instilling a Service Mind-Set

One of the most important features of Jane Stanford's message is that she never really defines "children." It was a shrewd decision, because as the university has grown from a local to an international institution, the scope of that term has grown commensurately. The university now sees its duty as service to the global community. All institutions, whether corporations, nonprofits, or government, should be engaged in the process of preparing the next generation of leaders. If we want that generation to view servant-leadership as the best path, we need to think how we develop a service mind-set.

At Stanford that begins with our own student body. The university's goal is to inculcate in all students both leadership and a dedication to serving others. Many Stanford undergraduates arrive with community service experience from high school. So how do we take that to the next level, encouraging students to use their rapidly growing abilities to the good, and introducing them to work opportunities in the public and nonprofit arenas?

The creation of an extensive, formal service-learning program began in the 1980s, with one of our former presidents, Don Kennedy, and Peter and Mimi Haas, who vigorously supported the idea with their counsel and philanthropy. President Kennedy created the Haas Center for Public Service, the first major university center devoted to service learning. As we approached the twenty-fifth anniversary of the center several years ago, my colleagues brainstormed about ways to take public service education and opportunities to a new level. The need for leadership in government, communities, and nonprofits was growing, but student interest seemed to be flat or even diminishing. Could we find a new method to engage students in deep and fulfilling service opportunities?

Out of this thought process came a program, championed by Professor Larry Diamond, called the Cardinal Quarter. This program enables students, through a small stipend, to leave school for a quarter, to go off into the world and learn by serving others, perhaps locally, perhaps in a major city or in Washington, D.C., or even in the developing world. When the program was first proposed, I was unsure how much student interest we would see. Would our students be willing to give up a quarter? To answer that question, Professor Diamond proposed a small pilot, which I agreed to fund. The pilot attracted more than twice as many applicants as we had opportunities, and subsequently donors responded with equal enthusiasm, enabling us to grow the program rapidly. My wife and I remain enthusiastic personal supporters of the program, and we hope to see a day when alumni talk about their Cardinal Quarter with the same passion that they talk about their freshmen dorm or their experiences studying abroad.

A second initiative, Seed, the Stanford Institute for Innovation in Developing Economies, began during this time as well. This initiative came out of the Graduate School of Business, with the backing of Bob King, an alumnus of the business school, and his wife, Dottie King, two wonderful people who care passionately about the poorest people on the planet. Seed's goal is to train business leaders in developing economies to end the cycle of global poverty by growing business and employment. Seed puts Stanford's expertise in teaching entrepreneurship to use in serving those most in need around the world. The newest Seed outposts opened in 2017 in India and South Africa, joining existing programs in Kenya and Ghana.

One doesn't often think of elite business schools as concerning themselves with the least well-off of society. Seed, however, has caught the imagination of both undergraduates and MBAs, who have lined up for internships to work with budding entrepreneurs and to help small businesses in these countries. The program has already enjoyed a number of successes, including one young woman who used her engineering training to solve a crucial problem in an African factory that extracted plant oils. In the process, she helped a struggling business, she stretched her own skills, and we all learned that the world is a much smaller place than we think.

This is service in its most fundamental—and most powerful— form. When you encourage and support this service mind-set in your own organization, the reach of your goodwill extends far beyond your internal constituents.

Recognizing the Service of Others

As a leader it is easy to get wrapped up in big projects and ambitious initiatives, and, in the process, to forget the smaller, but no less important, individual acts of service taking place all around you. Much of that service supports and enables the widely celebrated success of others.

At Stanford, we host a lot of ceremonies celebrating student and faculty accomplishments. Occasional Nobel Prizes, Olympic Medals, NCAA championships, major scholarships, and commencement all get their due. Award recipients step up on stage and draw the cheers and congratulations of the crowds, but what about all the people—the coaches, department heads, research assistants, employees, and staffers—who, in some way, contributed to their success? They quietly recognize their own service, or perhaps they get a pat on the back. At best, they'll get a mention in a recipient's acceptance speech. To their credit, they never ask for more. That's true service.

As a leader, especially a servant-leader, I believe I have a special obligation to all the people who serve. That's why I repeatedly appeared to recognize and congratulate the winners of Stanford's annual Amy Blue Awards. These awards celebrate the contributions and service of the staff members of the university. Not faculty members, not deans or vice presidents, but typically first-level or second-level staff who are nominated by their fellow employees. In their nominating letters, people write of their co-workers, "This person brings joy to our office. They're always there. They're excited. They're energetic." One recipient had worked for decades in one of the dorms, cleaning hallways and student rooms, always with a smile on her face. Another nominee had spent his entire working life on campus as a craftsman, making himself available to anyone who needed help. Another had started on a food service line and now oversaw one of the major dining halls. Most had worked at the university for two decades or longer, and they all took great pride in the accomplishments of our faculty and students.

I almost always attended this ceremony, to hand out the awards and shake the hands of the winners who were typically accompanied by family members and a cohort of co-workers. Why? Simple: I wanted to show the recipients that their work—their service—was important to the operation of the entire university. They helped make Stanford University a success. I also had a second, hidden, reason for being there: to remind myself of the people I *really* worked for, the folks I was deeply honored both to lead and to serve.

4

EMPATHY

How It Shapes a Leader and an Institution

"You never really understand a person until you consider things from his point of view. . . . Until you climb inside of his skin and walk around in it."
Atticus Finch, To Kill a Mockingbird, *by Harper Lee*

In the early 1990s, before I had assumed a major administrative position, I had the opportunity to act as an advisor to an extraordinary young woman in her first year at Stanford. The daughter of a migrant farming family, this young woman had spent most of her high school years moving every three to six months, starting in Southern California in winter and moving north to Washington for the apple harvest in fall. Despite the challenges she faced, she had excelled academically, and she was admitted to Stanford in a year when the admissions rate was less than 20 percent. I was awed by her determination.

Since her family clearly could not afford Stanford's tuition, she had received a full scholarship, including room and board. She graduated with a degree in engineering, but her story, one that Jane Stanford would applaud, stayed with me. It shaped my understanding of the value of an admissions process that considers an applicant's life journey, not just a person's grades and test scores. Further, she had earned her spot at Stanford, and neither the cost of attendance nor her family's financial means should have stood in her way.

Hence, financial aid became a passion for both the provost and me, and over the sixteen years we served Stanford, we managed to

expand the endowment for undergraduate financial aid by $800 mil-
lion, an increase of almost five times its value in 2000. Empathy
played a crucial role in our efforts to increase financial aid and, as
you will see in the next chapter, to protect it during the biggest financial downturn of the century.

It surprises me that many leaders, in academia and even more so
in business, still believe empathy should play no part in decision making. For them, the big decisions must rest on empirical facts, data, and
dispassionate judgment. It has taken a lifetime, but experience has
taught me otherwise: empathy should always be a factor in making
decisions and setting goals. Empathy represents a crucial check on
action—placing a deep understanding of and concern for the human
condition next to data can lead to decisions that support the well-
being of all.

Empathy cannot be calculated by an equation or confirmed by
a set of facts, and this is frustrating for an engineer like me. By the
same token, empathy is not something you can justify simply with
appeals to foundational documents, such as a mission statement.
Rather, empathy comes from the heart, which is what makes this
deeply human emotion both wonderfully meaningful and, if it is
misguided or allowed to overwhelm reason, potentially dangerous.
Nowhere is this truer than when one holds a position of power or
authority. It takes great skill—and inevitably some trial and error—
to find the right blend of emotion and reason.[1]

Generally speaking, people expect that nonprofits, including colleges and universities, will operate with more empathy than will corporations, from which stakeholders expect a direct financial return.
Nonetheless, what I have learned about leading with empathy in an
academic setting relates to any setting. No matter what kind of enterprise you lead, you will find innumerable opportunities to act with
empathy for employees or customers, for members of the local community, or for victims of disaster. Your challenge will be to choose

and shape the opportunities that make the most sense for you and your organization.

Empathy: Personal and Institutional

Taking the leap from a story that touches your heart to a full-fledged institutionalization of a response can be risky. In fact, it's better not to think of it as a leap, but as a series of well-considered steps. When a spark of empathy inspires you to action, you must ask yourself, does this warrant a personal response or an institutional response?

For example, years ago, in reaction to a disaster in another part of the world, a group of our students started collecting money to aid the victims. I was all in favor of their fundraiser, but when the students came to me proposing that the university match their donation, I paused. This situation provided a teachable moment. University funds mostly come from donor gifts and tuition paid by families. Both sources expect their funds will support the university's core mission of teaching and research, not disaster relief. So I told the students, "I'm not going to commit university funds, but I'll personally match the money you raise." In addition to respecting the sources of university funds, I hoped my actions would teach the students a lesson: empathy and charity are about personal involvement. This wasn't about me, as president of the university, taking money out of some university account. This was about my personal commitment to action.

On the other hand, during my tenure as president, some situations led me to consider an empathy-driven institutional response. For instance, I remember receiving an email from a young woman who had been admitted to the Stanford Teacher Education Program (STEP), an intensive, twelve-month teacher training program that culminates in a master's degree and a teaching certification. The program emphasizes preparing outstanding teachers to serve with longevity in underprivileged districts, where schools typically experience high teacher turnover rates. Many STEP graduates dedicate their careers to working in these environments, with children who are coming from difficult home situations, who are often one or two years behind their grade level, under the pressure of No Child Left Behind and with limited resources.

In the email, this prospective STEP student explained that she had grown up in Chicago, in an under-resourced neighborhood. She hoped to complete STEP and then return to her neighborhood to teach. Unfortunately, with the limited financial aid we offered her, she didn't see how she could handle the debt she would incur pursuing this degree, in addition to her existing undergraduate student loans, on a teacher's salary.

That got me thinking. Here was an individual who wanted to pursue an inarguably important, socially valuable path. She was ready to make her own sacrifices, signing on for one of the most challenging, yet most notoriously underpaid professions in our society. Should the cost of her education stop her from undertaking this critical role? This situation certainly called for critical consideration of an institutional response.

Since educating students who serve society is a goal for the university, I started thinking about how we could help this young woman, and others like her. It turned out that one of the major donors to our School of Education had a mother who had been a teacher, and therefore she understood deeply the importance of great teachers. Together we devised an equitable, sustainable, empathy-driven initiative. Combining some presidential discretionary money and her matching gift contribution, we built not a scholarship program, but a loan forgiveness program. When a STEP graduate teaches in an under-resourced, low-income school district, Stanford forgives a portion of his or her loan. If that teacher remains in the district for four years, Stanford forgives the entire expense of the graduate program.

Born of empathy and designed with reason, this program benefits STEP students and empowers STEP's mission. Both the university and the donor made a contribution toward resolving one of the biggest problems in our country, the quality of education, particularly for low-income children. This program also addresses a long-term challenge faced by elite institutions across the country, where undergraduate students from well-off families far outnumber those from low-income families. These institutions have not yet been effective enough in finding and attracting talented low-income students in reasonable proportion. It is difficult to build a bridge from these students to Stanford, in part because their school districts, often under-resourced, lack academic advising programs and struggle to retain talented teachers. Developing such teachers is the precise goal of the STEP program. If you view the university's mission as providing a path for people to get ahead through their own ability and effort, then an investment in loan forgiveness for STEP is a commitment to the university's core mission, both for the present and for the long-term future.

In the end, this initiative aided the rest of the university as well, because it taught us a new and valuable perspective: graduate schools typically look first to funding their PhD students. Instead, this was a professional program that trained teachers. It had a different role to play, in both education and society, and it deserved its own high priority.

Not to mention, it just plain felt good to help.

Empathy as a Learning Opportunity

I've come to understand empathy as both an occasion for an emotional response and an invitation to learn.

Whether you are leading a campus, a nonprofit, or a corporation, at any given time multitudes of people will ask for your help, appealing to your sense of empathy. Determining when and how to respond is one of the biggest challenges facing any leader. You can never fulfill all of these needs. You need a system, a kind of emotional triage, to help you decide where to put your energy and resources.

A series of questions can help. Does your heart lead you to this issue? Do you believe in it enough to take action? Would addressing the issue at hand fit with your organization's mission? If so, does your organization have the resources to help? If not, could you address it personally? Of the resources either you or your organization has available, how much do you want to dedicate to this cause, knowing that doing so will limit the resources available for other causes? Can you design an impactful, sustainable response to this need?

These questions can lead you to a deeper understanding of your own values, your colleagues' and your organization's reach, and the issues affecting people in your community and beyond.

Even after this triage process, you may find yourself facing a multitude of viable causes and having to choose only a few. In many cases, you simply have to develop the fortitude to say no. It is never easy. After all, you don't cultivate a strong sense of empathy just to turn down calls for help. The best you can do is to listen to your heart while using your head, plotting your direction with a combination of the two.

At a Stanford Commencement, Bill and Melinda Gates gave the most fascinating husband and wife talk I have heard. Bill thinks in terms of numbers and technology, seeking ways to solve public health problems around the world, for instance by using GPS to track immunization efforts, to ensure every village is covered. By comparison, Melinda reaches out to make personal connections, for instance, by visiting a hospital ward in India and holding the hand of a woman who is dying of AIDS. They are the living embodiment of both head and heart, and together they have been hugely influential philanthropists. We can do the same in our own spheres, when we integrate both head and heart.

Balancing Empathy and Equity

A problem that almost every philanthropic organization—or institution that practices philanthropy—faces is mission creep. They start out with defined guidelines about what they plan to give and to whom, but eventually the guidelines dissolve as the organization starts making donations to whoever has the most sympathetic story.

Universities forever face mission creep, especially when awarding undergraduate financial aid. At Stanford we serve a diverse group of students, with a broad range of family backgrounds. Therefore, in formulating our financial aid program, we wanted to create a system that extended opportunity to students from a variety of backgrounds, while fairly balancing how much families are asked to contribute. In other words, we wanted to balance empathy and equity.

Stanford has practiced need-blind admissions for many years. When students apply, we consider only their achievements and not their ability to pay. If they are admitted, we meet their financial needs on the basis of family income and resources. Despite this generous financial aid program, we noticed a failure to attract lower-income students, often the first in their families to attend a four-year college. Speaking with these potential students, our admissions staff quickly discovered part of the problem: sticker shock, combined with a lack of adequate college advising. (Research by Caroline Hoxby and others has documented this problem, called "undermatching.") Without someone to help them understand financial aid opportunities, students from families with low incomes simply assumed a school such as Stanford was out of reach.

To address this issue, working with the admissions office, the provost and I proposed a program in which students from lower-income families would get either free tuition or free tuition plus free room and board. We wanted to send a message powerful enough to shatter the perceived barrier between these students and Stanford. "Your tuition is $0" was the right message.

When we made the announcement, offering students whose families earned less than $100,000 free tuition, and adding free room and board if they earned less than $60,000 a year, a few people, mostly concerned alumni, responded with skepticism. "Well, I don't know that this is such a good idea," they said, "because you're giving them a free ride, and their education has value." Fortunately, our program already addressed this point. In fact, the students weren't getting a free ride; they would make a personal contribution using their income from working ten hours a week during the academic year and twenty hours a week during the summer. Once we shared these details, the skepticism melted. "Oh, that's reasonable," people said. When empathy contravenes fairness, it creates problems. Once alumni understood the personal obligation—however modest—they deemed the program fair.

The new program addressed fairness through a second provision as well, by including a change in financial aid for families with incomes above $100,000. Here we needed to make two considerations. First, we knew families above that income level were stretching to make the expected contribution (based on a federal formula) of $20,000 or more a year, and they were concerned about passing on debt to their children. Second, there was an issue of fairness: if a family making $99,000 a year paid no tuition, how could we ask a family making $101,000 to pay $10,000 or $20,000 a year? To solve both problems we had to adjust the financial aid commitment, so families with one child in college, with incomes between $100,000 and $160,000, could receive significant financial aid.

Once all these terms were clear, both alumni and faculty saw the program as a real commitment by the university to equity and opportunity. What truly impressed me was that the students who would benefit most from the financial aid program were not children of those alumni, who typically are quite successful. They were other people's children. So in addition to furthering Stanford's mission, the new financial aid program stimulated the empathetic nerve in many alumni. They merely needed to see that their empathy was acted upon with fairness and reason.

Empathy with Your Team

Empathy and fairness—ideally you will express these qualities in all areas of your leadership, not the least with your own team, the people who report directly to you.

In general, my team's appeals for empathy arose from two sources: a personal, often medical, issue, or a family-related issue. In both cases, I have espoused the same philosophy with everyone: "Your health and your family come first. Stanford comes after those two things. You have to deal with the personal issue first, and we'll make it work." At times this philosophy has resulted in temporarily reduced productivity, requiring the team to step up and fill the gap, but in the long run, in sixteen years as president, I never regretted it.

A second philosophy, however, led to some regrets. I treated my staff as responsible and capable adults, and I empowered them to manage their own time. They could decide when they came into the office and when they didn't. All that mattered to me was that they got their jobs done. Unfortunately, in a couple of cases, people took advantage of this policy—they weren't getting their jobs done and they were a drag on their team. Again, empathizing with their humanness, I told people, if it happens once, it's forgiven. After all, anyone could make a mistake, but if it happened more regularly, a call to fairness tempered my empathy.

Taking compensation for a job that one is not fulfilling is not fair to the university. Leaving others on the team to take up the slack isn't fair either. Nor is it healthy for team morale when one person doesn't contribute equally.

Under these circumstances, I had to tell the offending person, "You're not being the team member that we need here, and you need to clear this up or decide this isn't the right job for you." My regret is that in some cases I waited too long to have these conversations. It's not easy telling somebody they're screwing up, especially when some aspects of their work are exceptional. In the name of fairness, though, it's necessary. Still, I tried to communicate the difficult message clearly and with empathy.

In one type of circumstance, deciding to terminate a team member's employment is easy for me. If an employee acts out egregiously, intentionally bringing harm to others or to the institution, in my mind that employee has already fired him or herself. In these rare cases, my empathy still comes into play, but it is extended to the victims, the team, and the institution, rather than the offending party.

Perceptive Empathy

I think our sense of empathy is about to be severely challenged. The rise of artificial intelligence and machine learning is going to disrupt jobs and employment. This transformation could affect many different types of jobs, from robots and self-driving cars replacing manual labor and drivers to programs for medical diagnostics and treatment replacing radiologists and other physicians to AI-systems for automating legal and office work replacing paralegals or administrative assistants. I think this change is going to be at least as profound as the Industrial Revolution, and it's likely to move a whole lot faster, since software is much more scalable than large-scale industrialization. I believe empathy demands that we pay attention to those implications.

Everyone in a position of authority in our society will need to be sensitive to what's going to happen. Universities need to start thinking about the societal implications. Corporations participating in this revolution also have to help society adjust to this change.

We may see more and more people experiencing long-term unemployment or underemployment. We need to start thinking about those people now—not least because many may be our neighbors or co-workers. We need to realize that a shifting job market driven by radical technology innovation may lead to temporary unemployment, but it does not mean that the affected individual is unemployable. We have to think about jobs that didn't even exist before, as well as those that cannot be replaced by computers, no matter how smart. We need more teachers, and we need more people working with the elderly as our society ages—in other words, jobs in which the human element is deeply embedded and not reducible to algorithms.

As leaders and educators, we need to start right now preparing people for that work, and that education must include teaching empathy. It's that human element, the emotional connection and caring, that a human can bring and a robot or an app cannot.

Developing Empathy in Future Leaders

To prepare the future leaders of the world, as is the mission of Knight-Hennessy Scholars, we think it is important—indeed critical—that we help our scholars develop empathy. How can we foster empathy in others? This question calls to mind something I experienced on a tour of Lucille Packard Children's Hospital. Visiting children with congenital problems and cancer, I remembered watching my own son, at the age of three, suffering with a debilitating—and potentially permanently disabling—disease. I knew a little of what these families were going through, and that personal experience deepened my empathy for them.

In the Neonatal Intensive Care Unit, where premature newborns and those with major congenital problems are supported and treated, my empathy expanded beyond my experience. There I saw a pair of severely premature twins, so small I could have held one in the palm of my hand. Some people question the time, money, and resources that go into saving such tiny babies whose prognoses range from grim to hopeful. To many engaged in that debate, these babies' lives remain theoretical. I saw them with their mother who, despite the tangled wires, beeping monitors, and plastic incubators, was doing her best to pour maternal love into her babies. I knew then that trying to save those infants was the right thing.

We want our scholars to have that experience—to know that feeling of empathy and to be filled with a deep desire to make things right. Empathy usually implies compassion and perhaps charity, but we are looking for more than that: we are looking for the kind of empathy that changes people as a result of their interactions with each other, the kind of empathy that arises when one sees the world anew through someone else's eyes. Certainly we'll seek that quality in our candidates, but we'll also seek to strengthen it during their time with us.

Some of this training will occur incidentally, through scholars sharing their life journeys with each other. Some of it will be structured through in-person interactions with people in need. I still remember one of my visits to Stanford Charter School, where a young man spoke about what he viewed as one of his greatest challenges: making sure his younger sister had milk. Every day he would save the carton of milk that came with his free school lunch, bringing it home for her. He changed my perspective and strengthened my resolve to help.

We want our scholars to hear these stories and to realize this is happening in America, right here in Silicon Valley, one of the richest communities on the planet. We want them to realize that if it is happening here, it is happening everywhere. Our graduating scholars will be in the unique position of actually being able to make consequential change and alleviate human suffering, but only if they stretch beyond understanding that suffering and actually feel it.

Sara Josephine Baker exemplifies this elevated empathy.[2] As a physician in New York City in the early twentieth century, she saved perhaps hundreds of thousands of children's lives by creating a children's public health agency. The anecdote that opens her autobiography suggests that empathy was driving her actions long before she became Dr. Baker. A young girl from a well-to-do family, Sara Baker once saw a little black girl walking down the street in rags. Shocked by the sight, she propelled herself to action, taking off her own clothes and giving them to this girl. Reading that, one thinks, "This person is going to grow up and change the world." She did, making profound public health contributions to the immigrant community in New York and, her most important legacy, fighting for urban children and newborns living in poverty. That is the kind of empathy we want to cultivate in our scholars.

It's one thing to visit a hospital or a school in an economically challenged neighborhood or a homeless shelter. It's another thing entirely to open your heart to the people you meet there, to allow yourself to be changed by the experience. We hope our scholars will let this deep empathy guide them, as leaders dedicated to creating positive change in the world.

5

COURAGE

Standing Up for the Institution and the Community

"It often requires more courage to dare to do right
than to fear to do wrong."
Abraham Lincoln

Humility, authenticity, empathy, service-mindedness—these characteristics shape a leader's vision and chart a course toward right action. Courage, on the other hand, compels a leader to take that right
action. While many people can discern what is right and true, acting
on that discernment is more difficult. The leaders who practice courageous action are ready to transform their organizations in necessary, significant, and lasting ways.

People often conflate courage with bravery. Certainly they are
connected: acts of bravery usually require an underlying courage, and
a courageous life is sometimes made manifest through acts of bravery.

To my mind, courage is continuous, a character trait that serves
as a foundation to a life of decisiveness and moral direction. Bravery,
however, is incident-based, a willingness to take enormous risks during
those brief moments when they need to be taken. A soldier storming
a pillbox on Omaha Beach on D-Day is incredibly brave; that same
soldier, now permanently injured, requires courage to get through the
subsequent years of pain, disability, and reinventing his life.

Most of us in academia and in the corporate world experience
few occasions that demand bravery. Courage, though—that's an-

other matter. In small and large ways, the courage in our character is tested regularly. As a leader, you may need to draw on personal courage to respond to events outside your organization, such as a natural disaster or a national tragedy. You also may need to call on your courage to address internal events, to take necessary risks, to change your position, to admit a mistake, or to recover from a failure.

To different degrees, each of us has that courage in our character. How much we're willing to exercise it, I believe, is a product of how many times we've flexed and strengthened that muscle in the past. Courageous people are no less fearful than everyone else; rather they've learned to live with their fears while taking right action. As anyone with gray in his or her hair (or white, in my case) knows, the learning curve is long and punctuated with moments of terror. Yet acting with courage gets easier with each lesson.

The layoffs at MIPS, my first few public speeches as president of Stanford, and as you'll see, the events surrounding 9/11 and the recession of 2008—these experiences taught me that demands for courage from a leader are often greater than from the people they lead. That said, leaders also enjoy certain advantages that help them bolster their courage. Four pillars helped bolster mine.

Remember the Core Mission

When facing a real challenge in a leadership role, people have a tendency to personalize that challenge, to make solving it their own private quest. From my experience, you will solve few such challenges that way. Rather, you are more likely to become overwhelmed, to let your emotions and passions get in the way, and to lose perspective and objectivity.

In difficult times, I found it helpful to remember that the challenges were not about me as a person, but about my role as the leader of my organization. Behind me stood an institution with a developed philosophy and values; history and precedent; and a team of dedicated, loyal people. When you face troubling circumstances, aligning what you do with the core mission and values of your institution will become critical. It puts the steel in your spine.[1]

After the financial crash of 2008, hewing to Stanford's core mission provided valuable support as we executed on a controversial decision. With my provost (the university chief academic and budget officer, and my right-hand person), I explored whether we needed to make a major cut in the university's budget or to suffer the death of a thousand cuts extended over a decade.

Many of our colleagues urged us not to make significant cuts, but to spend down the endowment instead. Given the size of the losses we had already seen (almost $5 billion—over 25 percent—of the endowment had vaporized by spring of 2009), we knew we needed to make cuts. We doubted the incremental trim approach would solve the problem, not to mention that the thought of trimming annually, for seven to ten years, was stifling.

Presuming the economy would recover slowly, we chose to make a major cut, all at once. Though carefully thought-out, the decision still felt like a risk. What if the economy recovered quickly? Then we could be blamed for a preemptory decision that led to layoffs, frozen salaries, and a halt on faculty searches that would leave the university stumbling in the talent race with our competitors.

Once we decided to take that risk, we met the next phase of the challenge. We had to decide who would bear the burden of those layoffs, in an economy that might offer few chances of finding other employment. Initially we thought we would ask each unit to take the reductions equally, as a fraction of their budget. Before we did that, though, we considered our core mission. Were there areas we shouldn't cut?

What's most important in a university? Students and faculty. Simply put, we decided we could not fire faculty members (although we did freeze faculty salaries) without suffering an enormous blow to our reputation and undoing a decade of successful recruiting. Further, in keeping with our core mission, we could not cut financial aid to our students. How we would manage this was another matter entirely.

During the good times in early 2008, we had announced the largest increase in financial aid in Stanford's history: students from families earning less than $100,000 per year would be able to attend Stanford tuition free (see Chapter 4, "Empathy"). Simply maintaining that commitment would require making additional cuts of about $20 million in recurring annual expenses. (Ultimately the situation would become worse than we had anticipated, since the economic downturn meant that many families had less income available for tuition, so they requested additional financial aid, amounting to about $5 million annually, a shadow effect that lasted about five years.)

As you can imagine, the decision to maintain financial aid while forcing administrative staff to suffer the impact of layoffs was a hard one to swallow. It meant that university employees, many of whom had been loyal members of the Stanford family for years, were going to bear the pain, while students—some of them not yet attending the university—were still going to receive their scholarships. Surprisingly, no one voiced an objection to this decision, and I think that reflects the dedication and values of people who work in a university.

Once we had made these decisions, we needed to communicate both the seriousness of the situation and the unfortunate but necessary actions. Because we felt it was important that the leadership "lead," the provost and I both took 10 percent salary reductions, and we asked the deans and vice presidents to take voluntary 5 percent reductions. Set against the bigger financial picture, the savings from these cuts were small, but we did help save a few jobs, and we underscored the fact that we were all in the same boat.

Looking back, do I have any regrets? No, but you can never really forget the human costs. Hundreds of people lost their jobs, and while we tried to be as humane as possible in the process, increasing severance packages and enhancing retirement options, I know we lost good people who suffered. The quick action we took (quick, at least for the academic world) meant we recovered sooner, we could begin hiring faculty again, and we even managed to rehire some of the talented people who had been let go. In the end, while making decisions that cause people pain never feels good, our direction felt sure because it was guided by the university's core mission, and that gave us the courage to proceed.

Step Up When the Community Needs You

During a football game, players look like the embodiment of power: knocking helmets, high-fiving, roaring over triumphs and defeats. However, inside the locker room before a game, something very different happens. It's tense, quiet, even anxious, as team members run important plays through their minds, readying themselves to perform for the next three hours. Similarly, I've met great actors, known for their dramatic emotional range, who are understated and soft-spoken in person. I know CEOs, dynamic in front of their constituents, who are shy and introverted offstage. My point? No one is "on" all the time, but as a leader, knowing when to stand up on behalf of your community, whether in writing or in speech, is critical to your role, and doing so takes courage.

From the looks of it, most leaders feel comfortable in front of a crowd. They seem always to know what to say and how to say it. Behind the scenes, though, they have to tap into their courage to rise to the occasion. They have to work hard to make it look easy. How do they do it? When leaders focus on speaking not as themselves but as a voice for their organization, they become the embodiment of the institution, and thus they speak with a power and confidence they would never have speaking just for themselves. Remember, your institution has enough confidence in you to have made you its leader, so no matter how personally frightened or nervous you may be, you can speak from that confidence and from that duty.

I remember three key moments when speaking up for my community stretched me beyond my personal capacity and grew my courage.

As I began my presidency in 2000, Stanford was working on its General Use Permit, the agreement with Santa Clara County that allows the university to build new buildings, make use of its lands, and even to operate. Silicon Valley was booming at the time, as was a small but vocal antigrowth movement. Just as the university was proposing its ten-year plan for slow growth (relative to the pace of growth in industry), the antigrowth voices were rising. When the long permit application process culminated in a final hearing with Santa Clara County supervisors, I was tasked with kicking off the conversation by describing the university's plan. In the few minutes I was given to speak, I focused on sharing our new research directions, enumerating our educational plans, and introducing planned facilities that would benefit the broader community. I was about halfway through when one of the county supervisors interrupted me, saying, "This work is all fine, but Stanford is also a large land developer making lots of money through the development of unrelated projects." I froze. My blood pressure spiked. I could have lost my temper, but on behalf of my community, I composed myself and said, "Mr. Supervisor, the university is a nonprofit organization. Every cent that comes from those projects is used to fund research or provide scholarships for students who otherwise could not attend Stanford." My words met a rousing chorus of applause. Rather than getting lost in my own frustration, I had found the courage to stand up for what mattered about the university.

A few months later, in the aftermath of 9/11, I found myself speaking in front of the Stanford community, not because I wanted to, but because my role as president required it. I am a native New Yorker, born a few miles from Ground Zero. I knew people who lived or worked nearby, and I knew that members of the Stanford community had lost loved ones and friends. When Stanford held a memorial service in the main quad, along with the leaders of our various religious communities, I was asked to address the crowd. I knew I could set my personal feelings aside and rise to the occasion, because it wasn't John Hennessy who needed to speak; it was the president of Stanford University. My community needed to hear comforting words from their president, and that gave me courage.

My first concern, of course, was to honor the victims of the tragedies in New York, Pennsylvania, and Washington, D.C., but I was also worried about backlash against Muslim students and citizens. So I centered on an excerpt from Lincoln's second inaugural address:

> With malice toward none, with charity for all, with firmness in the right as God gives us to see the right, let us strive on to finish the work we are in, to bind up the nation's wounds, to care for him who shall have borne the battle and for his widow and his orphan, to do all which may achieve and cherish a just and lasting peace among ourselves and with all nations.

It's hard to go wrong when you quote Lincoln. In the second inaugural, he reminds us that the right and courageous action is not seeking revenge, but acting with compassion and working for peace.

Four years later, I found myself once again compelled to step up in support of members of my community. The president of one of the country's great universities had opined publicly that perhaps biological differences were responsible for the underrepresentation of women in science and technology. His remarks were meant as an invitation to explore the relationships between intrinsic differences and societal effects. However, they were interpreted differently and taken up by pundits as carte blanche to express views that women were not as skilled or as capable as men in math and science. (We find ourselves in a similar situation today, in which the comments of some leaders have emboldened racist, Islamophobic, and anti-Semitic groups.)

Our women colleagues—both at Stanford and across the nation— were deeply offended by these developments. In discussions with knowledgeable researchers, I had learned about the significant issues of implicit and explicit bias that were disadvantaging girls and women in pursuing careers in science and technology. I felt I needed to support my colleagues and to provide a different perspective. Speaking out to criticize a colleague, even indirectly, is rarely done in the academic world, but I concluded that it was the right path. Together with Susan Hockfield, president of MIT, and Shirley Tilghman, president of Princeton, we wrote an op-ed to try to make it clear that increasing the representation of women in these fields was both fair and important to the country. More than a decade later, this struggle continues, as evidenced by the famed "Google memo," containing similar opinions about biology and ability. While our op-ed certainly helped, as hundreds of emails testified, clearly it didn't end the debate.

Sometimes you will need to speak out to carry the voice of your institution, but that doesn't mean your rhetoric will carry the day. On numerous occasions, I spoke out in favor of the Dream Act, a change to our immigration laws that would create a path to citizenship for undocumented young people brought to the United States as minors. Many "Dreamers" attended Stanford and other universities, and we felt they deserved a future in our country. Alas, neither I nor my many colleagues who spoke on the topic succeeded in convincing enough politicians on both sides of the aisle to embrace the cause. Yet courage means being willing to try—and to continue trying— even if you may not succeed. Creating lasting social change requires persistent action, across generations. Even if you don't realize the end result you seek in your lifetime, you can find courage in the fact that you are changing people's lives for the better along the way.

If you can free yourself from your own ego and become the voice your institution or your community needs, though your hands may be trembling when you step up to the podium, as you open your mouth, your fear will abate. As I have experienced it, the transformation is amazing: a minute ago I was uncertain about my duty; now suddenly I know exactly what to do. That doesn't mean you don't need to prepare your message, edit it ruthlessly (make it shorter, more precise, clearer), and practice it endlessly (assuming you have time—crises have their own clocks). Lincoln spent quite a while getting the 272 words of the Gettysburg Address just right. Practice, practice, and more practice developed a knock-kneed Mark Twain into one of the greatest public speakers of his time. If you focus on the needs of your audience first, you can trust that you will stay on course and your courage will find you.

Sometimes Courage Means Standing Firm

In contrast to a situation in which the community needs you to speak out and the challenge is finding the right words, you may find yourself in situations in which a group of people demand that leadership speak out or take action, when you know that the advocated speech or action would violate a core principle of the institution, would be unfair to individuals, or would have negative consequences for the institution. In these moments you may feel enormous pressure to speak out, but you have to find the courage to stand firm.

Perhaps the most difficult situations we faced involved student protests. The students had noble intentions but were often uninformed or misled by individuals seeking to mobilize them. In political settings, where protests are common, or corporate settings, where they are rare, the primary technique used to handle protestors is to avoid encounters by isolating the leadership from the protestors, often using security personnel. In a university, where the protestors are usually students, isolation is not an option. The leadership must be willing to meet with the students, as well as to endure shouting, chanting, and name calling (including, for example, a poster labeling me as the worst boss in Silicon Valley). Other tactics included occupying the reception area of our offices (armed with kitty litter to use to relieve themselves), engaging in hunger strikes, camping outside of our building, effectively blocking the entry, and arriving at my personal residence at 5 a.m. with a chanting crowd (including hired protestors) who blocked the street and threw a rock through a window.

These protests were typically accompanied by a list of demands that students wanted us to agree to immediately. I have to admit that I was occasionally tempted to take the easy path out and simply agree, but that would have been a mistake both because agreeing to the demands would have harmed the institution (and sometimes others) and because it would have set a terrible precedent. Instead we needed to find a way to listen to demands, to discern the right action, and to stand firm with our decisions. A few examples illustrate the range of challenges we faced.

One of the first extended protests I encountered, undertaken primarily by students advised by union personnel, demanded living wage rules for subcontracted workers. The protestors' tactics included public demonstrations and a student hunger strike, and they insisted we implement a universal policy, which we deemed inappropriate, since we did not think it could be implemented or maintained. The student hunger strike worried me deeply. I was concerned for the students, and while I thought we were doing the right thing as an employer, the depth of the student's protest made me uneasy.

In meeting with some of the workers, we identified two legitimate issues: one involving an unfair interpretation of a policy on temporary workers, and the other involving the use of a subcontractor with a poor labor relations record. In the end, we adopted a policy designed to fix these problems, but we stood firm on other key issues. I learned from this experience not to assume that all parts of a large organization are living up to the standards you might expect. In the end, even though we limited the focus of our policy, one of the companies that ran several dining establishments catering primarily to students concluded that the required policy would make it uneconomical for them to continue operating. Their workers were laid off. Stanford dining services took over the facility, but they had to raise prices to accommodate their higher salaries, causing a number of students to complain about the cost of food. Beware unintended consequences.

Other demonstrations and marches demanded modifications in union contracts, prior to bargaining discussions. The goal of these protests was to obtain concessions before formal negotiations began. On these issues, we simply stood firm, refusing to negotiate contract terms outside of the bargaining process.

A more complicated issue came to our attention when students, protesting the use of sweatshops in manufacturing Stanford-branded athletic wear, staged demonstrations and a building takeover. Since subcontractors in the developing world typically did the manufacturing for the major athletic brands, and universities had no direct connection to the subcontractors, some of whom have negative records as employers, our course of action wasn't immediately clear. The students demanded a variety of solutions, including isolating all manufacturing of university athletic wear in "model" factories. Unfortunately, their proposed solution would have had a negative influence on the monitoring of the factories where 90 percent of workers were employed, since monitoring would be concentrated on model factories. We could not agree to this demand, since we saw it as a step backward; we did agree to join two agencies involved in monitoring these factories.

Perhaps no issue in recent times has been more difficult for colleges and universities than the issue of sexual assault. Three aspects of this issue pose challenges: in the vast majority of cases both the victim and alleged perpetrator are students, universities are ill-equipped to handle what is a potential criminal investigation and prosecution, and confidentiality for both the survivor and the alleged assailant means that the broader community rarely has a full picture of the events. Bound by these circumstances, we could do little to appease student protesters demanding that we override decisions made by university judicial boards in cases involving alleged sexual assault. Overturning a judicial board process that attempts to weigh all the evidence in a confidential hearing, and imposing a punishment demanded by a partially informed crowd, would be unjust.

Unfortunately, we could not defend our decision by discussing the confidential details of these cases, even after one party had made a partial disclosure. On some occasions, the media significantly compounded the tensions by oversimplification and by one-sided or distorted investigation and reporting. We knew attacking the students or the press would not be fruitful. At best, we could indicate that not all the facts were known, reiterate our concerns and sympathy for the survivors, and stand firm in support of the careful, deliberative process undertaken by the judicial board.

No matter the details of their protests, students are the core of the university, and they typically have virtuous motivations, including compassion and justice. Despite their partial understandings of the issues at hand, there was always some truth and righteousness in their uprisings. Hence, I learned the importance of making sure I had the facts right, of listening to their viewpoints, and of understanding the consequences of both existing policy and the demands to change policy. Once we had a complete picture, we could summon the courage to make a change or to stand firm.

Don't Be Afraid to Take Risks

Even if you do not experience demands for change in the form of public protests, you can be sure that change will assert itself on your organization. New challenges are constantly emerging, and what might be considered success is forever evolving. As the leader of an organization, you may believe it is your job to maintain the status quo, to convince others that the best course is the safest course. You may set out primarily to protect the assets of your organization, as you are its ultimate guardian. You may even convince yourself that prudent stewardship and holding the line against fads is itself a form of courage.

Well, perhaps, but not for long.

In the fast-moving twenty-first century, the overly cautious are soon rolled over by the speeding wheels of change. Effective modern leadership is driven by the ability to manage and grow an organization in an environment of continuous change. This means not only activating the courage to take well-calculated risks, but also learning to navigate the cycle that follows risk, quickly and decisively recovering if a risk fails, or capitalizing on its successes. Further, even if risk-taking is against your nature, for the good of your organization, you must find the courage to practice it. As the leader, you set the behavior pattern for everyone you lead. A risk-adverse leader's behavior can undercut innovation and the sharing of new ideas throughout an organization.[2]

Of course, being a risk-taker has its own challenges. A reckless CEO could lead a company in the wrong direction. More commonly, a chief executive can encounter resistance from institutional stakeholders who don't want to see change, either because they are doing well with the status quo (often managers and supervisors), because they are afraid of losing what they've got (often investors and lower-level employees), or because they have a thoughtful disagreement with the new direction. This last group should never be ignored, because they may be—at least partially—right.

In the end, though, it is your job as leader to decide whether or not to take a risk. You may improve your chances of success by doing your due diligence, and you may minimize the likely backlash by educating your stakeholders on the benefits of your strategy, but in the end the decision is yours.

If your decision leads your organization to success, you get to celebrate the team that helped you get there. On the other hand, if you realize you've steered your organization in the wrong direction, you need to find the courage to admit that fact and change course, ideally minimizing your losses. The deeper you are into the process, the more courage it takes to reverse yourself. You may suspect I'm speaking from experience here. I am.

In the summer of 2011, New York City announced plans to build a campus for a university outpost, on Roosevelt Island. The campus would emphasize science, technology, and entrepreneurship, and the university that partnered with the city would receive a space on the island, along with $100 million to jumpstart the project, most of which would need to be spent just preparing the site.

When the city invited Stanford to make a bid, I was intrigued. Stanford has many small facilities in its network of exchange and research programs, but none are major outposts, and typically they have no permanent faculty. This New York City project could allow us to add a wholly new campus, housing both teaching and research, to expand the university's two core missions.

What other great university has a first-quality, full-service campus located a continent away? I knew embarking on this endeavor would be an enormous risk. It struck me, however, as a vehicle to take Stanford to the pinnacle of twenty-first-century institutions. We could tie together two of the great power centers of the world—Manhattan, the heart of banking, art, and communications, with Silicon Valley, the heart of technology. It would provide unequalled access and opportunity for our students and faculty, and it could be a powerful recruiting magnet, attracting top-notch faculty members who wanted to live on the East Coast or in a great metropolis.

Before taking the leap, I surveyed the Stanford community and found that the two most important parties, my faculty colleagues and the trustees, were split over the idea. Among the university's trustees, some were very enthusiastic, but others thought the risk too great. After all, we were just coming out of the recession, so they were reluctant to launch immediately into an expensive new venture. They worried that an effort in New York, estimated to cost nearly a billion dollars for phase one, and double that over its lifetime, would come at a cost to the Palo Alto campus. I understood the concern, but I disagreed with it—now was the perfect moment to take advantage of our restored momentum and to position the university for the rest of the century. I conveyed this message, and I held firm.

Further, some trustees were concerned that the city's selection process would become political in the end. While their concerns had given me some doubts, the mayor had assured me the selection criteria would be merit-based, not political. I communicated this assurance to the trustees, agreeing that we would walk away if it became a political battle.

Among my faculty colleagues, quality was the biggest concern. They feared we would create a symbolic outpost in New York, a B-grade campus unworthy of the Stanford name. I understood this valid concern: creating a lesser campus would undermine Stanford's status and divert resources in doing so. So, we further developed the plan by making the new campus on Roosevelt Island equivalent to the Palo Alto campus, right down to the faculty and graduate students, who would be shared between the two locations. We would have one university in two locations, not two separate institutions. The possibility of hosting undergraduates studying for a quarter in New York City added to the appeal. Once the faculty members understood the nature of our plans, they largely supported the endeavor.

The selection process moved to a final round, with Stanford and one other candidate in the running. Our negotiating team was working hard with their counterparts across the table; the deal was getting favorable coverage in the media; we had formed a partnership with CUNY, both for a temporary home and a long-term relationship; and the trustees visited Roosevelt Island to see for themselves the potential of the site. All in all, it looked like we had a good shot at closing the deal.

At this point, scores of people had devoted thousands of hours to the project, the whole world was watching the selection process unfold, and I had put my reputation on the line, convincing tens of thousands of people in our community to believe in the vision, converting detractors into committed supporters. Then negotiations began to fall apart.

Admittedly, we had seen early warning signs that everything was not entirely as it had been represented. At first, we chose to ignore the signs—after all, risk-taking requires a nearly unwavering belief in your vision. Typically in negotiations involving nonprofits, one side shares everything the other side needs to know. After all, you aren't competitors; you are two organizations engaged in a common mission. Our negotiations with the city were different. Throughout the process, our investigations turned up new revelations, most notably the presence of a waste disposal area (and likely environmental hazard) under the old hospital that occupied the site of the future campus.

Making matters worse, the New York team asked that we pay market value for the land on which we were planning to build housing for faculty and students, as if we were a profit-driven real-estate development company, rather than a nonprofit university providing housing to students and employees, at rates below the cost of construction.

As these revelations and requests amassed, the question begged to be asked: What do we do now? We wanted this deal to happen. We had spent a million dollars on the proposal alone, and we had used the combined brainpower of some of the most seasoned people at Stanford to develop it. Despite our growing concerns, we decided to continue the negotiations, aiming to limit the risks and pitfalls.

Then the city demanded we guarantee a certain number of faculty members and students at the new campus, on a timeline, as a contractual obligation. I understood their goal was to ensure that we would achieve their aims. However, meeting this demand would undermine a key principle of the project, that the Stanford faculty would control faculty hiring and student admissions, and we would not sacrifice quality to quantity.

That's when I decided: this is just not going to work. This contract would violate the university's core values. No matter how badly I had wanted this deal, no matter how real that new campus had felt to me as I was standing on the proposed site, seeing Manhattan just three hundred yards away, I had to change course. I called a meeting of my staff, my general counsel, and our VP of land and buildings. We examined every detail, including the various alarms triggered in our negotiations with New York City and the attendant risks if we did sign the contract and could not meet its terms and obligations. Our fears were confirmed. I would not subvert our core mission, or undermine our values; thus I would not sign that contract.

Perhaps the city's negotiators did not understand that a university operates very differently from a real-estate developer. They had added on conditions, believing we were so hungry for the deal that we'd accept them. They did not realize—and perhaps we had failed to communicate clearly—the depth of our commitment to our vision and to the university's underlying values.

When I called the chair of the university's board of trustees, Dr. Leslie Hume, to tell her we were pulling out of the New York deal, she was surprised, but not for the reason I had expected. She told me she had worried that my team (meaning I) had become so committed to the deal that we would go ahead with it no matter the obstacles. I think she was relieved to hear the news.

I suspected the repercussions of walking away from the deal might be significant, that we might be eviscerated in the pages of the *New York Times*, but I didn't lose a minute's sleep. In the end, we received mostly affirmations and kudos from both our New York alumni and the New York press. At home, the trustees who had been the strongest supporters of the project understood why we walked away. The faculty members were relieved we hadn't sold them out to make our dream come true. Indeed, by showing the courage to pursue such a high-risk deal—and then the courage to walk away from it—we reinforced the notion that the Stanford community supports mindful risk-taking and respects bold, value-driven action.

Personally, I have no regrets. We had been right to take the risk, and in the process to envision what a university might be in the twenty-first century. Equally, we had been right to walk away from the deal when it violated our fundamental principles, when the concerns of the doubters had become reality. Within a week, even as the newspapers were still covering the story, I began to look for new opportunities to effect a similar transformation, maybe one that would make an even greater impact on the world. That quest eventually led to the vision for Knight-Hennessy Scholars.

Though you may need to let go of a dream, when you lead with courage, your efforts will not be lost, and you may be pleasantly surprised by what you gain.

6

COLLABORATION AND TEAMWORK

You Cannot Do It Alone

"Coming together is a beginning, staying together is progress,
and working together is success."
Henry Ford

Collaboration—teamwork—is not something we always associate with great leaders. After all, being the boss means you don't have to partner, you get to command, right? You didn't strive to become the leader just so you could share authority with others, did you? If there are to be teams, it will be because you order them; you don't join them.

In my experience, the opposite is true.

Leadership is, in fact, all about collaboration and teamwork. Sure, certain tasks you will complete on your own, but most significant endeavors will be accomplished by a team—your team, not one you order into action, but one in which you actively participate.[1]

This may not be news to you. Here's what may be new: your team members are your equals, and in terms of contribution, some will be your superiors. I've seen too many teams in which the boss is not only the leader but also the ruler whose contribution must be recognized before and above everyone else's. That's not a team—certainly not a successful team—but a petty tyranny. For me, the classical model, *primus inter pares*, or first among equals, has produced the best results.

An effective leader needs to know not only how to participate on a team, but also how to build a team, how to motivate its members, and how to foster an environment that supports creative thinking, in which team members can make the kind of nonlinear, non-incremental contributions that lead to great outcomes.

That said, in all honesty, I'm not sure that I'm a born teammate. Rather, I credit science and technology for turning me into a dedicated collaborator. These disciplines taught me to play well with others and to appreciate that two or more minds, working with synergy, are usually much more powerful than one.

Living and working in Silicon Valley and at Stanford have reinforced that belief every single day. In these settings, I have learned that it usually isn't the leader but often the most junior member of a team who ultimately makes the most insightful contribution. This happens for a number of reasons: youthful energy, greater willingness to take risks, recent exposure to the latest innovations, an anti-authoritarian attitude, less fear of losing one's reputation, and freedom from precedent. Both high-tech companies and academia understand this phenomenon, which is why they make a continual effort to break down boundaries, both within and across teams. The elimination of vertical and horizontal walls allows a graduate student, a new junior employee, or someone from an adjacent team to make key contributions to a project.

Dismantling hierarchical thinking isn't easy. It is human nature for people with more experience and higher rank to resist sharing authority with a junior colleague who holds a lesser title. This "flattening" of authority happens a bit more readily among scientists and engineers, though, for two reasons. First, the natural sciences have a long history of young people making important discoveries, often more so than their elders. Remember that Einstein was twenty-six when he had his *annus mirabilis*. In terms of individual contributions, scientists and engineers often peak between their twenties and their forties, so most senior scientists accept that the "kids" are going to make some real breakthroughs, while the elders will find other ways to contribute, often as a mentor, team leader, or facilitator.

Second, science and engineering are quantitative: we can objectively measure and assess the strength of an idea. We keep careful records of experiments, so if a team member complains about the results, or about who gets credit for what, we can turn to the evidence.

In less empirical activities, however, such as marketing, product design, senior management, or strategic planning, assessments aren't so clear. What should we measure? How can we measure it? Successes can have many mothers and fathers, and their contributions may be a matter of considerable dispute. Not surprisingly, in these environments, hierarchies can reassert themselves if they go unchecked. The boss and the intern know their place, and that can be bad news, because a junior team member may have an amazing insight, but it will be lost if people pull rank.

It is vitally important that your organization's culture encourage equitable opportunities to contribute. That culture begins with you, the leader. When you humble yourself enough to become a true team player and you honestly value the contributions of others, you set the course for success.

Building Effective Teams

In addition to modeling collaborative behavior, to create successful teams a leader must select the right participants and set ground rules for the team's operations. These tasks may not be as straightforward as they seem. I learned a great deal about them through my participation in the MIPS project, which began at Stanford in 1980.

Our investigation started with a very simple question: It will be possible to build complete computers on a single chip. Should they be built differently than just copying minicomputers or mainframes? In recognition that we were developing something fundamentally new and unproven, we set out to assemble a multidisciplinary team, to guarantee we would identify all possible scenarios. We needed people who could design integrated circuits, people who understood computer organization and architecture, and people who understood compilers and operating systems. Finally, because we had only a small team to design a microprocessor and its core software, we needed people who could build their own computer-aided design tools to give us leverage.

Our team included myself and a few faculty colleagues who would provide context, organization, some specific knowledge (for example, I was the initial compiler expert), and judgment. The rest of the team members were graduate students. We anticipated they would provide most of the key ideas. They thought in terms of novel approaches, in a cross-disciplinary fashion, trading off whether a necessary capability would be provided in hardware or in software. These were exactly the young, bright minds we needed—willing to revisit and reinvent the conventional wisdom. They were independent, critical thinkers.

Faculty members were tasked with establishing the process for our investigation. We would begin by brainstorming about the problem: the whole team would read the relevant literature; then we would offer ideas for consideration. While we encouraged new thinking, these ideas could not be completely unconstrained—if they were, the process would never end. They were bounded by reality and accompanied with some insight into why they might make sense. Setting those boundaries would be the job of us "old-timers," the faculty. (I was twenty-eight at the time.)

As Jeff Bezos has captured with his two-pizza rule (that all meetings should be small enough that two pizzas should feed everyone), small, highly effective teams are more efficient. We had exactly that kind of team—a tight group of top-notch thinkers. In addition, research has shown that the most productive teams contain the maximum diversity of skills, viewpoints, and personalities. How do you maximize team heterogeneity, while at the same time holding the team together? This is the ultimate challenge to the leader of any such team.

The multidisciplinary nature of our team created its own set of challenges. When you bring together talent from different perspectives, you must equally empower each member of your team. Otherwise the team is likely to break down into cliques, typically among people who share the same technical vocabulary. In addition, because the credentials of members from one discipline may be different from those of another, hierarchies can form across the disciplines, with one group believing its contributions to be more valuable or necessary than another's.

Certain ground rules circumvented interteam rivalries. First of all, I reminded everyone of our shared goal: we wanted to achieve something great. To make it great, all pieces of it had to be excellent. This established a basic respect for the expertise of all members on the team.

Further, to support innovative, cross-disciplinary thinking, I set a second ground rule: at the start, we don't criticize ideas. Instead, we think them through and evaluate them without judgment on the source or prejudgment of the idea.

To this I added a third ground rule: tough questions aren't only allowed, they are necessary. They must be asked with respect and received with openness, and only then will they be evaluated. If a team is going to accomplish anything important, ideas must be challenged vigorously, even ruthlessly. Those challenges must be focused on the ideas, not aimed at the team members who offered them.

This led to my final ground rule: team members must be treated with the utmost mutual respect. After all, if we weren't good enough to be part of the team, we wouldn't have been invited into it. Especially in a group made up of alpha-status individuals, team leaders must quash the notion that the person who speaks the loudest wins. Instead, you must cultivate a work environment that encourages thoughtful debate while discouraging personal criticism or anger. On the MIPS project, the faculty members modeled and enforced this behavior.

The lessons I learned participating in the MIPS project, and subsequently in Silicon Valley, became important practices in my leadership as Stanford president. In particular, I tried to use the same ground rules for teamwork. I encouraged new ideas and tough questions. I never shot anybody down for bringing to the table a problem that needed attention. On the contrary, I might excoriate them for not bringing a problem to the table. I wanted team members to feel safe saying, "You know what, John? I think you are about to make a mistake." I needed team members who weren't afraid to speak up.

Knowing Your Role: The Key to Successful Collaboration

I have been involved with many teams and collaborations in my career, but two of the most important could not have been more different from each other. Therein lies another lesson for effective collaboration: you must find your part and play it.

This is why my partnership with Jim Clark, which began when I was still a professor and researcher, worked so well. Upon meeting Jim, it was clear to me he was out to change the world. A born risk-taker, he wasn't afraid of making mistakes or of offending those who didn't agree with him. He seemed almost incapable of thinking small, and he didn't listen much to advice. While some people found Jim challenging to work with—he was as intense and demanding as he was brilliant and charismatic—I rarely had any trouble. In fact, we worked together well. Why? Two reasons. First, I appreciated Jim's dedication to big things and his commitment to success. He was in to win, and so was I. Second, I quickly found my role and stuck with it: Jim had the big vision and the core ideas to enable computer-generated graphics, and I built the tools that helped him achieve his vision. I learned a lot along the way, which laid the groundwork for MIPS several years later.

Fifteen years on, as president I found myself in a new and very different partnership, with John Etchemendy. In character, he is the antithesis of Jim Clark. Both are men of stellar intellect, but Etch is diplomatic, measured, and the most patient person I have ever known.

Etch was a professor of philosophy at Stanford. As a logician, he had a fair amount of expertise in computing. I had worked with him briefly on a university commission on technology in teaching, and I knew he was a deep thinker, interested in the future of the university. Etch had been the co-chair of the search committee that chose me as president. I, in turn, had asked him to be provost, the university's chief operating officer.

Many provosts take the job because they see it as a stepping stone to the presidency. In the role, some discover they don't enjoy large-scale university administration. Others find that provosts, who often control faculty appointments and budgets (the coins of the realm in academia), simply make too many enemies. As a result, a provost's tenure lasts an average of four to five years. Etch stayed in the job for over sixteen years—longer than any other provost at Stanford. What contributed to his longevity? For one thing, he did not aspire to be a university president. More important, he excelled at the job, mastering the complexities of a $5 billion operation while minimizing the number of enemies he acquired.

Our partnership worked well for many reasons. We both knew our roles and played them. I was Mr. Outside, to Etch's Mr. Inside; I was the public visionary, while Etch navigated the ship. Unlike in my partnership with Jim, in which we each had to be careful not to step on the other's turf, there were almost no boundaries between Etch and me. In many situations, we were all but interchangeable. I never hesitated to send him in my place to any university meeting, function, or event. I knew he would represent the office of the president as well as I could, and that any position he took or message he offered would accurately reflect my own opinions. Etch and I trusted each other completely.[2] I knew I could rely on him both to handle complex issues and to share with me everything I needed to know. I was able to serve as president of Stanford for sixteen years in large part because of my partnership with Etch.

Collaborating to Achieve Something Remarkable

Early in our terms as president and provost, Etch and I ran into a big problem. Stanford needed to replace its football stadium, built in 1927 and significantly out of date. The project would be costly, and its financing needs would conflict with the needs of the major academic initiatives we were about to launch. We didn't see how we could undertake the project, and we needed help. So we called John Arrillaga, an alumnus and a former member of the basketball team, who had been a significant supporter of Stanford athletics over the years. John also happened to be one of the most success- ful commercial real-estate developers in Silicon Valley, having mastered the art of constructing buildings both quickly and cost effectively.

John stepped up with a solution: he would contribute to and help fundraise for the new stadium, but he also wanted to determine the stadium's final design and to head up the construction process. Under normal circumstances, no organization would hand control of a vital asset over to a volunteer, especially not on a project with a likely budget of $100 million or more, and several members of both our staff and the trustees expressed concerns. Etch and I, however, had developed a good working relationship with John in the past, and we trusted him to do the right thing for Stanford. Were there remaining doubts? Of course, but we concluded that the risks were justified. Hence our collaboration began.

On Thanksgiving weekend in 2005, at the end of the last game against Notre Dame, bulldozers rolled onto the field to begin con- struction. On September 16, 2006, less than ten months later, Stanford played Navy in the new stadium. John Arrillaga's design exceeded what we had hoped for, and unlike many college athletic stadiums, the project was completed without significant debt.

In the succeeding decade, John, who became known as Mr. A, undertook many projects for Stanford, including student residences, three fitness facilities, additions to the basketball arena, new playing and practice fields, and a new office for admissions. Throughout my presidency, he contributed to and oversaw the construction of several dozen capital projects. This unusual collaboration, in which a donor is intimately involved in the design and construction of projects, is far from typical for an institution's capital projects, but it has certainly worked out well for Stanford. The partnership continues today. After I left the presidency, Provost Etchemendy and Mr. A agreed that he would contribute to and build the largest student residence on campus, a desperately needed facility, given the soaring rents in the Bay Area.

We sought a different kind of collaboration with the Anderson family (known by their nicknames Hunk, Moo, and their daughter, Putter), in an effort to strengthen Stanford's offerings in the arts. Over the years, the Andersons had assembled one of the finest private collections of modern American art. Thanks to the education efforts of my spouse, I was familiar with the work of many of these artists, including Pollock, Rothko, Diebenkorn, Guston, Francis, Thiebaud, de Kooning, Oliveira, Motherwell, and others. My predecessors had talked with the Andersons about donating parts of their collection to Stanford in the past, to no avail. I decided it was time to try again, but with a new team of Stanford people. Bringing the Anderson collection to Stanford would transform the quality of our art collection and help raise Stanford's profile in the art world.

A group from Stanford started meeting with the Andersons. We knew the Andersons had devoted their lives and their life's earnings to assembling that collection, now worth hundreds of millions of dollars. We learned that they wanted to house the collection in a place where it could be displayed together and would be looked after with care. Could we find a way to build that home on the Stanford campus? I was worried about the costs of building and maintaining a home for the collection, especially since it appeared that the money had to come largely from the university's core budget. Nonetheless, we continued our discussions. When it became clear that the collection could really come to Stanford, we found a number of close friends who believed in the importance of the arts and understood the transformative power of the addition of this collection. They contributed to help us construct a building, and today the Anderson Collection at Stanford University is something the campus community and visitors from around the world share and enjoy.

As these projects illustrate, collaboration is much more than a few personalities teaming up and working together, hoping the chemistry will balance out. It is rather like a marriage—you make compromises and adjustments toward the overall goal; you face doubts and resolve them together. Neither of these collaborations was typical of academic-style collaboration—in both cases we were working with tough-minded entrepreneurs who had built major companies, and in both cases we achieved something no standard academic collaboration could have achieved. By thinking outside the normal structure of relationships, by building truly collaborative teams, and by aligning our interests, we were able to achieve remarkable things.

Collaborating up the Chain

So far, we've discussed the collaboration that leaders initiate with their staffs, and collaborations that extend beyond the boundaries of their organizations, but most of us also have bosses, so we need to learn how to collaborate upward.

During my years as department chair, dean, and provost, I had individual, direct supervisors. Learning to collaborate with them was important to my success in those roles. Equally important, by reflecting on how my superiors encouraged and challenged me to stretch for my goals, I learned how to be a more effective mentor myself.

When I moved into the presidency, formally the board of trustees became my boss, a group of thirty to thirty-five people, with the lead role played by its chair. I worked with four spectacular chairs: Isaac

Stein, Burt McMurtry, Leslie Hume, and Steve Denning. They performed the dual roles of engaging their fellow trustees in the work of the board and in being the chief board partner for the president. They not only put in many hours during their four-year terms as board chair, but also all traveled extensively as we engaged in a variety of fundraising and alumni outreach events.

The university board operates in much the same way as a corporate board of directors (except trustees are volunteers).[3] Of course, the board has a fiduciary oversight role and may need to step in when the actions of the leader are not serving the institution well. Most of the time, however, the board and leadership enjoy a collaborative relationship. The board supports the CEO, acting as advisors and using their own knowledge and skills to enhance the work of the management team. Likewise, the CEO's job is to keep the board informed—"no surprises," we used to say—and to engage the board in discussions about major decisions and strategic directions, gaining wisdom from the board's perspective.

The key to a successful collaboration with the board lay in two principles: in knowing and respecting our roles and in mutual trust. The board understood that its role was not to manage or run the university; that was the job of the leadership. Similarly, the leadership knew that the board had ultimate responsibility for appointing and evaluating the president, for protecting the reputation of the university (a shared responsibility), and for ensuring the institution's long-term financial health. The trustees are the guardians of the interests of future generations. Understanding these roles allowed us to build a trust relationship: I was honest and forthright with the board, and while we certainly engaged the board on virtually every major decision, I trusted that they would listen to and support the decisions of the leadership team.

In a nonprofit such as Stanford, the board plays another major role: it is a source of both philanthropy and fundraising, giving and soliciting the gifts that enable the university to thrive. In such efforts, the collaboration between the board and the entire university leadership team is crucial to success. In the next chapter, "Innovation," we'll see how a major collaborative effort among the academic leadership, with a group of current and former board members, created, fundraised for, and executed a ten-year strategic initiative for the university.

The Team Leader: Choose Well and Then Be Ready to Help Out

As a leader, eventually you will find yourself not only participating in the teams you create, but also delegating team leadership to others. This presents a whole new set of challenges, perhaps the most important of which is choosing the team leader and helping him or her succeed. How do you choose the right person? Who can you trust to recruit a talented team with the right interpersonal chemistry, to establish a respectful and productive team culture, and to draw the best performance out of each individual member so they reach their collective goals?

At first, this transition can feel vulnerable. Presumably you reached your position in part because you are a good team leader and member, and now you must entrust that job to someone else. How do you know that person will carry the mantle well? They say great ballplayers often struggle as coaches or managers, because they compare their players' performance to the skills and drive they themselves had exhibited. Similarly, in recruiting a team leader, you may find yourself rejecting candidates because you doubt they could perform at your level. Sometimes this assessment is accurate, but just as often you are seeing your own past through a rosy lens. Remember, it took time for you to develop the skills you have, and you likely stumbled more than once along the way. Take caution to look not for the person who will do the job in the same way as you, but for the person who has a history of positive collaboration and who exhibits the leadership characteristics necessary to get the job done.

Once you have chosen your team leader, you must step back and allow this person to do his or her job. The danger, of course, is that you might judge the leader's actions, thinking maybe he or she is doing a B+ or A− job, but you would have done an A+ job. You may even feel tempted to intervene, to save the leader from making avoidable mistakes. Unless the dysfunctionality in the team is obvious not only to you but to those around you—and especially to team members—you must resist that temptation. Team leaders make mistakes. That's how they get better. Whether or not you remember, that's probably how you got better too.[4]

Trust your team leader, and trust your own judgment. In your role as executive, you don't have the bandwidth to micromanage your appointed leaders. That said, if you see—or if others call your attention to—a project sliding off course, you will need to intervene.

Sometimes intervention means coaching a struggling leader. Often asking the right questions can illuminate key issues the team leader needs to consider: Is the team converging? Have they identified clear opportunities and challenges? Do they have a plan for engaging wider support? I encountered several situations in which the team leader and the team core had a clear vision, but they had not engaged the broader community, without whose support the effort could not succeed. If you have picked the right person and you ask the right questions, your team leader will get the message and address the issue.

If coaching doesn't correct the course, you need to assess the options for replacing your team leader. Do you have time to act as interim team leader, while also recruiting and onboarding a replacement? If you cannot devote the necessary time and effort, changing leadership may prove more destructive to the team than maintaining the status quo.

On a few occasions, I have launched new efforts even though I suspected the leadership was weak. Sometimes you may feel like you don't have a choice: the institution has an immediate need or you see an opportunity that requires swift action. In such circumstances, I chose the best available leaders, but the team didn't gel, or the process moved too slowly, or the leader failed to attract or inspire team members. When you have no one better to take over leadership, you need to make the hard decision: cut your losses and move on. In such cases, I have tried to end the effort gracefully, declaring a partial victory, letting the team claim some success, while diverting resources to more worthy projects with stronger teams. In the next section, we'll discuss dealing with a failing collaboration.

Handling a Collaborative Effort That Doesn't Work Out

Team collaborations can fall apart for a number of reasons, beyond the choice of the team leader. Sometimes an initiative falls apart because the visionaries behind the initiative don't find the support they need from the institution, or because their rationale for the initiative was as not as compelling as they thought it was. What happens when our best efforts go awry? We need to remember our humility.

I encountered such a situation in 2007, when we proposed to expand the size of the undergraduate class. Surveying national trends, I saw that demand for the top universities, both public and private, had soared. In 2007 Stanford had received more than 25,000 applications for the 1,650 places in the freshmen class, an increase of almost 50 percent since 2000. In the preceding twenty-five years, selective private institutions had grown very little, most of them less than 5 percent, while applications had more than doubled. Although public institutions had grown, most were facing financial difficulties due to diminished investment by states; they could no longer be counted on to meet the rising demand.

To me, expanding the undergraduate class felt like a moral imperative: Stanford could find the resources to grow, and we had an extraordinary pool of applicants; therefore we had a responsibility to try to accommodate more outstanding students. I set up a faculty-based task force—chosen from people whom I thought would both support the expansion and contribute their own views to our exploration. I also began to talk to the trustees about it.

The moral imperative argument failed to sway a number of people. To them, adding a few hundred graduates a year wouldn't really solve the problem. A second concern arose among a few trustees and a number of faculty members on the task force: some parts of the undergraduate experience needed attention, especially pre-major advising and residential programs. They believed we should commit resources to "perfecting" the undergraduate experience before investing in expansion.

Both the provost and I disagreed. We thought the experience of our undergraduates was already incredibly good. It wasn't clear that spending more money would make it better, at least not in a cost-effective manner. However, the opposition was entrenched. Could we have simply steamrolled the opposition? I suppose so, but it would have broken our trust relationship and undermined our ability to pilot future initiatives that required support from the faculty.

In the end, the financial crisis, which started just as the final task force report was being completed, gave us a convenient exit. We set the expansion idea aside for another five years. When we returned to the idea, we met no opposition, and we found a way to excite donors both about the expansion and about improving advising and residential life, simultaneously.

In hindsight, the failure of our initial effort was partially my fault. After all, the provost and I had picked the task force members, established the framework, and set them to work. Nonetheless, putting the expansion idea on the back burner for several years was the right thing to do, and it could be accomplished with minimal loss of face for everyone, given the financial crisis. Sometimes, no graceful exit offers itself, as we experienced in negotiations with New York City (see Chapter 5, "Courage"). In such cases, and especially if going forward without clear support could damage important relationships, future initiatives, or the well-being of your institution, you need to find the courage to admit your mistakes and move on to other opportunities.

Celebrating Shared Success

When collaboration works well, when a team reaches or even exceeds its goals, often team members don't want to see it end. In fact, the way you end is almost as important as how you begin.

In a successful team, you have helped convene a group whose members have found a way to work well with each other despite their differences, who have set out in pursuit of a goal and achieved it, and who have made an important contribution to the larger enterprise. These assets are gold; you want to preserve and expand them as best you can. You may want to work with these team members again, not least to bring their glow to other teams. You may also want to promote some of the most capable of these team members to leadership roles in teams of their own. How can you achieve this?

In a fast-paced work environment, the tendency is to shut down successful teams abruptly with a simple thank you for their work, or worse, to let a team deflate on its own, with its members dribbling off alone or in small groups. Rather, as one of the great lessons of human culture suggests, successful team efforts should end in celebration and ceremony—a gathering in which each member is recognized for his or her contribution, and the accomplishments of the entire group are placed in context and honored.

It is easy to dismiss such celebrations as mere retirement parties, but they are meaningful opportunities. As you are the person overseeing the team, your orchestration of this event is one of the most important contributions you can make in a team's story. You are telling all of them, from the leader down to the most junior member, that they are important, and that what they accomplished was valuable.

During the time I served as president, my wife and I hosted many dinners in our home, from annual thank-you events for the academic and administrative leadership to celebrations of major gifts to the university. In the final year of my presidency, we decided we wanted to do something special for the volunteers and supporters who had been crucial to our shared success over the sixteen years we had served.

So my wife and I decided to host a set of thank-you dinners, inviting former trustees, some key volunteers and advisors, and those who had helped launch and support some of our most important initiatives. These dinners were our way of saying, "What we've done at Stanford over the past sixteen years is a shared accomplishment, and you've made important contributions, helping make Stanford better for its students and its faculty. It would not have happened without you."

At these events, with all attendees' attention, I would go around the room and thank each person individually for something particular they had done to support our success. I wanted everyone to know how their specific actions had made the institution better. I wanted them to hear that their efforts mattered and I appreciated them, deeply.

It was a wonderful set of dinners, during which genuine gratitude and shared goodwill elevated all our spirits. Isn't that what collaboration is about? Becoming more as a team than you ever could be alone? Why wait until those important people—your teammates—have moved on before you notice who they were to you? Why not celebrate your time together while you are still a team?

7

INNOVATION

The Key to Success in Industry and Academia

"To succeed, planning alone is insufficient. One must improvise as well."
Isaac Asimov

We've all heard the old adage that the only thing constant is change. Thanks to innovation and the digital revolution, the speed of change has increased. In Silicon Valley, we have felt that acutely for a half century. Now the rest of the world is feeling it, too, and we see no indication of that pace slowing anytime soon.

While we're all feeling the effects, the nature of change isn't monolithic. It differs, for example, between the commercial world and the academic world. I have experienced these differences first-hand, having worked in both worlds, at Stanford and in the tech industry. Across my career, I've seen a pretty full palette: from starting a company and cold selling a new idea to investors, to helping take a company public, to serving on the board of several organizations that have shaped the technology landscape, to backing start-ups as an angel investor, and from the everyday work of a university faculty member to leading an institution with several thousand faculty members, tens of thousands of students, a multibillion-dollar annual budget (the total revenue of the university and its hospital subsidiaries would put it in the Fortune 500), and an endowment of tens of billions (total assets roughly equal to Costco's).

Despite the central role of innovation and change based on innovation, in both academia and industry, these two worlds operate very differently. A failure to recognize that difference can be dangerous. Run a company like a university, and you risk oblivion; run a college like a company, and you will likely face a faculty mutiny. Nonetheless, both types of institutions must innovate to survive.

Freedom to Innovate

Much of the difference between academia and industry has to do with time horizons and risk-taking. In my experience, in the university you see more "far out" innovation driven purely by curiosity or serendipity. Why? Generally speaking, academics are not up against a deadline, rushing to market to beat the competition, nor are they at risk of losing their business if they fail to do so. Indeed, academics are not trying to design and fabricate a complete solution; instead they are striving to advance a field or to demonstrate a new idea. So they have the leisure of following curiosity, even allowing serendipity to happen. Rather than pressing toward next quarter's income statement or next year's product, the academic time horizon opens the door to fundamental research, work that can change the world. In fact, a revolutionary contribution in the future is much more highly valued than an incremental contribution today.

Three decades ago, when we started the MIPS project at Stanford, we knew we were in a new era of miniaturization, thanks to semiconductors and Moore's Law, and we knew that a wealth of opportunities were opening up. Intel and Motorola had both shown that one could take an established minicomputer architecture and shrink the design down onto one or two chips. This new chip—the microprocessor—was already transforming the tech world.

At Stanford, what we saw was that, as revolutionary as the microprocessor was, the initial versions were a contrived solution. Both Intel and Motorola had rushed to market—Intel to fulfill a contract to a Japanese partner—and had made many compromises along the way.

By comparison, we didn't have to make those compromises, or worry about compatibility; we could start nearly carte blanche. That was one of the perquisites of working in a university laboratory. We had the luxury of asking the big questions; for example, what if the way minicomputers, even mainframes, were designed was not the right way for microprocessors?

The result was the MIPS reduced instruction set (RISC) computer architecture. It would prove immensely influential in both the computer and the computer game console industries. In fact, it is unlikely that you haven't used a device in your life that incorporated a MIPS-based chip, at least if you're over twenty-five.

Would the commercial world have created something like MIPS? Perhaps, eventually, but we were able to design a more innovative and complete solution from the start, and that proved vitally important to the design's adoption.

Needless to say, being free to do as we pleased also greatly increased the odds that the MIPS design would be an utter failure, or just too impractical ever to find a real-life application, and many engineers in industry thought that our university prototype could never be scaled up to be a "real computer." Therein lies the point, though. At a university, you can take these kinds of risks, demonstrate a basic advance in knowledge, and be rewarded for that risk without much downside. On the flip-side, research that leads to incremental improvements does not receive much attention.

Innovation Drives Start-Ups

I can't tell you how many times I've had this conversation with students: the student opens with, "I want to create a start-up." I ask them to tell me about their technology, and they answer, "Well, I don't have it yet, but I want to do a start-up!" I remind these students that great start-ups begin with great technology discoveries (or at least novel applications, such as eBay or Airbnb or Uber). Innovation presents great opportunities for smart entrepreneurs, not the other way around.

A university research environment allows great freedom for innovation, in that academics are largely untethered from many practical considerations. There are countless areas of research attempting to answer open questions, such as what happened in the first microseconds after the Big Bang. While these questions are compelling, some of these research projects will remain simply interesting while others will lead to important discoveries and practical applications. It's not easy to predict *a priori* which will be which. Indeed, only a small set of these research opportunities are likely either to advance significantly the state of knowledge or to be applicable immediately in the creation of new products or companies.

Out in the business world, the expectations are very different. The marketplace enforces a narrower range of options and a much higher cost of failure. One may be rewarded for an invention that is only an incremental advance, but one won't be rewarded for any advance that doesn't sell. In this world, innovation means building something people will want, even if they don't know they want it yet.

One of Steve Jobs's core philosophies was that he didn't ask his customers what they wanted, because it wasn't their job to invent the future. It was his job. We see his approach made manifest in the iPhone. I'm not sure anybody knew how much they wanted a smartphone until they held one in their hands. Remember, cell phones and handheld personal assistants both existed, and many people had one or both devices. Jobs put them together in one device, and suddenly everyone needed an iPhone.

This is a hallmark of innovation. I was lucky to have seen some of the first demonstrations of Yahoo and Google. Both were true "Aha!" moments for me—Yahoo because it showed me that the World Wide Web would transform our lives, not just help scientists and technologists communicate, and Google because I saw a much-improved search engine, with a much better algorithm than anything in the marketplace. These are the products and services that succeed—the ones we never realized we needed until we had them. Now we can't live without them.

Partners in Innovation

The real power of academic and commercial symbiosis lies at this interface between ideas and implementation. Because graduate students and faculty enjoy the freedom to explore, radically new concepts and serendipitous ideas emerge from universities. Those ideas can sit idle until someone recognizes real-life, potentially profitable applications for them. The role of venture capitalists, government agencies, and ambitious entrepreneurs is to carry those ideas across this interface and make them real products and services that benefit humanity.

Google is perfect example of this. Before Google we had Alta Vista, a pretty good search engine, certainly a lot better than what had come previously. When two Stanford students, Sergey Brin and Larry Page, looked at Alta Vista with youthful eyes, they saw an opportunity. With a new algorithm and near obsession with getting the right result, Sergey and Larry created a significantly improved solution. Joining in their effort, Google CEO Eric Schmidt understood the importance of user trust, which would distinguish Google's search engine from others.

In particular, Google chose to drive search results on the basis of user interest and not advertiser interest. The search drove the ad selection, not vice versa. This same transparency and trustworthiness is reflected in Google's celebrated home page, which might have been sold to advertisers but was instead stripped down to simply asking the user to plug in his or her search terms. That decision in conjunction with a better search algorithm enabled Google to capture much of the search industry.

Though the innovations behind these companies germinated in an academic setting, the choices made by leadership in these companies, among the most successful in business history, probably would

not have emerged from an academic setting. Simply put, the expertise necessary to bring a discovery or new technology to market lies
beyond the scope of academic research, but it is crucial to the success of a product in two ways. First, we really cannot understand
all of the issues we will encounter in bringing a discovery to market
until we do it. Second, the choices we make in that process—the
complex trade-offs and decisions—can influence outcomes as much
as the impact of the initial discovery does. In short: academia and
industry need each other.

Academia and Industry: Finding Synergies, Transferring Discoveries

In an ideal world, industry and academia would recognize their differences and work to complement each other. In reality, bridging
that gap is difficult.

Universities have a hard time transferring technology, from deciding which discoveries have real commercial interest to making
the process friction-free. Universities are conflicted: they see technology transfer as an important part of their task, but they also see the
opportunity to generate much-needed revenue. Hence the growing
number of university-based venture funds, entrepreneurial incubators, and research commercialization initiatives—all of them targeted at helping the entrepreneurs while also securing a stake for
the institution. Indeed, the drive for dollars has even led to several
universities suing companies, arguing that the company should have
licensed a patent belonging to the university.

On the other side, corporations are caught in a challenging position. Many industries no longer fund basic research, finding the
returns too elusive and often too far away. Meanwhile, larger corporations grow increasingly frustrated by their inability to remain
innovative while agile start-up competitors run rings around them.

The result is a growing—and probably economically necessary—
overlap between these two worlds. The irony of course is that these

two cultures are largely incompatible. The corporation that wants to create a university-like research lab soon grows frustrated at the apparent aimlessness of the researchers in that lab. Before long the company begins demanding that researchers start producing something that will generate revenues. The university that goes too far trying to get its researchers to become more commercially relevant quickly discovers that it is no longer producing any fundamentally new discoveries.

As a university president, I tried to strike a balance: ensuring that research stays open, that the research benefits the public, and that—if there are financial returns—the university shares fairly in those returns, with the goal of using such resources to support future research. I suppose my trajectory as an academic with experience in Silicon Valley positioned me to make such decisions. I cannot speak for others, but I can tell you what I did.

On the basis of my experience in the Valley, I came to the conclusion that Stanford's role was primarily to foster the initial discovery or invention, and to educate students about how to succeed as entrepreneurs. Given the wealth of resources surrounding the university—from legal assistance to angel investors to VCs—Stanford could add little through incubators or similar proactive, tech-transfer interventions, at least in the information technology sector. (There may be opportunities in the biotech sector, where funding is harder to get and specialized and expensive lab resources are required.)

That said, a university could do a lot to block the creation of new ventures, either by limiting the ability of faculty and students to become entrepreneurs, or by making the process of licensing university IP financially or bureaucratically burdensome. It's surprising to me how many universities invest heavily in incubators but still restrict participation in start-ups or extract excessive royalties or equity. We took the long-established position at Stanford that the role of a university was to create a supportive environment for new ideas, and that the role of technology transfer was to transfer technology, not to try to extract all the blood you could from the founding team.

Moreover, I personally believed that since most university research is at least partially government funded, if the university invents something that could be useful in peoples' lives, it has an obligation to try to put that discovery to use. That's a moral obligation, independent of financial incentives, which might also exist.

Now I must admit that taking this moral position has had its practical advantages. Because Stanford has always allowed its students and faculty to pursue their commercial or entrepreneurial dreams, it has become synonymous with start-up success and therefore a mecca for college-bound entrepreneurs. That success has bred more success—because we consciously remove any barriers to it.

Managing Innovation: A Guiding Hand

How do you maintain an environment that is innovative over time? Here in the twenty-first century, this is the most important question every leader in every sector of our society, from industry to education to government, must continually ask.

From my perspective, an innovative environment begins with amazing people—creative thinkers who take risks and do radically new things. Once you have found your people, as a leader your job is to get out of their way. Great companies and great universities are hotbeds of innovation, but only when they allow creative thinkers to decide where the next opportunities exist.

The leadership team might identify and prioritize strategically important areas, such as genomics, machine learning, or new energy technologies, in which they see clear research opportunities and potential for significant societal benefits. However, this strategically focused research requires a light touch. You must refrain from providing a highly detailed, prescribed roadmap for your people to follow. Instead, you need to allow for serendipity and discovery. After all, you aren't the expert in their fields. They are.

Of course, the desire to control is natural. After all, you want a new investment to succeed; you want the big breakthrough to happen. If you try to assert governance over it, though, you're likely to stifle innovation. No matter how smart you are, the people you are working with are likely smarter than you, at least in their fields of expertise. Even if they aren't as individuals, ten of them working together certainly are. This line of thinking is captured in the 20 percent time guideline articulated by Larry Page and Sergey Brin in their founders' letter: "We encourage our employees, in addition to their regular projects, to spend 20% of their time working on what they think will most benefit Google. This empowers them to be more creative and innovative."

Prescribing 20 percent of your employees' time to creativity may seem like a tremendous waste of time and resources, especially when it's applied to a company with tens of thousands of employees, many of them in nontech jobs. But it is, in fact, a serious attempt to deal with one of the tech industry's greatest challenges: How do you stay innovative as you get bigger and more successful?

Lots of organizations are innovative when they are new. Innovation is, after all, the reason they exist. At a certain point, though, usually after an organization goes public and reaches a certain size, leadership begins to focus more on protecting assets, driving current products deeper into the marketplace and serving investors' short-term interests. Too often, when that day arrives, companies—even in places as dynamic as Silicon Valley—choose to take the less innovative course, even if it means serving short-term needs in exchange for long-term stagnation or decline.

Leaders in this position have solutions available, but they are usually so risky and onerous that few companies are willing to try them. Better, they think, to improve short-term ROI and enjoy the rewards in improved stock prices and earnings now (after all, that's what they were hired for), and to leave dealing with noncompetitiveness and decline to their successors.

One leader who chose a different route was Steve Jobs. He actually made Apple more innovative, but he began with several "advantages," if we can call them that. First, Apple Computer was in serious trouble when he reassumed leadership at the turn of the century. It was already in decline after years of lackluster innovation, so stockholders and customers were open to taking risks. Moreover, being Steve Jobs, he had already created over the years his image as a dedicated innovator, so employees, investors, and customers expected more of the same. Finally, from the day he returned, Steve set about educating the world, preparing people for a company that was going to dedicate itself not just to product innovation but to category innovation—a nearly unprecedented level of creativity, especially in big business history. Even so, ten years elapsed between his return and the transformative introduction of the first iPhone.

Can other corporate CEOs match Jobs's precedent? Probably not. Steve was *sui generis*. They can, however, borrow from his recipe for success, promoting innovation in their companies, rewarding it, and embarking on a campaign of educating stakeholders to be prepared for it. Most of all, they need to convince their own senior executives and boards of directors that the status quo is not enough.

Of course, adopting innovation as a strategy also means encountering and overcoming failures. For Steve Jobs: the Lisa was a failure before the Mac was a success, and NeXT was never successful as a personal computer. Personally, I had several serious setbacks in building MIPS as a company, and our effort to develop a campus in New York as well as the expansion of the charter school did not work out as planned. Embracing innovation means accepting and recovering from failure. The challenge is to avoid as many failures as possible and recover from the others as quickly as possible.

Innovation via a Strategic Plan

So far, most of our discussion of innovation, as well as collaboration, has been focused on a single project or initiative. How can one bring innovation to crafting a strategic plan that charts the development of a new set of activities and renews an organization? In the commercial world, these transformations occur when whole new product lines are developed: the IBM 360, the Apple Mac, and Google's YouTube. In a university, such efforts are often part of a continuum that involves a strategic plan and an accompanying fundraising campaign. For Stanford, rejuvenation came in the form of the Stanford Challenge and its successful fundraising accomplishments, the end-product of a multiyear planning effort to catapult Stanford forward.

In the preceding chapter, we noted that successful teams give equal weight to the ideas and judgments of their least senior or credentialed members, but that inclusiveness extends in another direction as well: to the diversity of knowledge, experience, and personality within the members of the team. This is especially true when one is developing an inherently cross-disciplinary strategy.

In some respects, multidisciplinary inclusion is trickier. It's one thing to listen to a junior team member whose knowledge at least comes from the same field; it's another to give standing to someone whose expertise lies elsewhere, perhaps even in a field that has little in common with the topic at hand. Yet some of the most important insights I received came from people with "outsider" perspectives. Let me explain.

In 2002, we first began discussions on what would become the framework of the Stanford Challenge, our development and strategic plan for the next twenty-plus years of the university's story. The previous fifty years of the university's history had been unequalled by any other comparable institution in the world: Stanford had leapt from being a university that often was omitted from the top twenty in the United States to one consistently listed in the top five. How could we match, much less top, that achievement?

The first thing we had to do was to ask how that had happened. It wasn't mere coincidence. Something drove that change. What was it?

Kathleen Sullivan, dean of the law school, gave us the answer: "There was a series of brilliant investments made," she said. "Growing engineering and the sciences, moving the medical school down from San Francisco to the main campus, and expanding basic research in the biosciences. Building the Stanford Linear Accelerator, the world's largest atom smasher at the time, and then using its capability to win a handful of Nobel Prizes. Those were all big, strategic bets, and they changed the whole future of the university."

This was not the kind of contribution one expects from the dean of the law school. Nonetheless, perhaps because of her outsider's perspective on Stanford's investments in the sciences, and because of her incredible eloquence, Sullivan both perceived and articulated the situation in a way that everyone immediately understood.

Dean Sullivan's remarks didn't just open our eyes; they gave us a new way to see our challenge. In recognizing the huge bets our predecessors had made, we were liberated to think big ourselves. We put together a rough outline of our now more ambitious strategy, and we began to organize committees from different parts of the university. Of course, our first task was to find great leaders for those committees—leaders that would allow new directions to flourish but also ensure that the committee produced a plan rather than wandering aimlessly.

Although multidisciplinary and collaborative research and teaching were our overarching themes, we needed planning committees to flesh out the plan by addressing particular areas where we saw potential. Thus we formed groups to explore opportunities in the environment and sustainability; in biomedicine and human health; and in international relations, security, and development. Stanford had some great leaders in each of these areas—leaders who could form the foundation for a larger effort.

With these areas named, the provost and I began thinking beyond them, to include disciplines that may seem less connected. One area, identified by a faculty planning committee, was the arts. Compared to our longer-established, East-Coast peers, Stanford was not as strong in the arts. We lacked a high-quality performance space, our museums weren't comparable, and the arts-practice components of our departments were small. Fortunately, we did have world-class documentary film and creative writing programs on which to build.

The provost and I were personally influenced to embrace the arts by our spouses, who had backgrounds in creative writing and visual arts, but what would the deans think of an initiative in the arts? How would we convince them?

This time it was the dean of the business school, Bob Joss, who surprised us, saying, "The arts are an intricate part of a great education, and they are an important part of the lives of our MBA students." Who would have expected that to come from the dean of the business school, of all places? That insight about the role of the arts across the university community led to a major initiative in the arts.

These contributions, from Deans Sullivan and Joss, were not only important in their own right, they also served as models for everyone else. Open your eyes, they said. Get out of your head. Don't just advocate for your own turf, but think about the needs of the university as a whole, and of its future generations of students. To clearly communicate this cross-disciplinary collaborative focus, at the event that kicked off the fundraising effort for the Stanford Challenge, the deans all spoke not about their schools, but about the initiative as a whole and its interdisciplinary implications.

Pulling a Strategic Plan Together

Once the academic planning groups and deans had coalesced on the strategic plan, the next steps were to develop the external vision and to begin communicating that vision. A small group of current and former trustees was convened to oversee and advise leadership throughout the process. This group acted in a fashion similar to how a corporate board would review a long-term plan for a company—providing perspective, asking tough questions, and clarifying directions. That effort came to fruition with a weekend retreat in Deer Valley, where we defined the two core themes: multidisciplinary research focused on the world's most challenging problems and the education of future global leaders who could put such solutions to work. The arts initiative was a key part of educating leaders who could be creative, deal with ambiguity, and possess a broader cross-cultural understanding.

That group then participated in a series of twenty-three campaign discussions held in a dozen cities in the United States and Europe. That process further refined the contents and the high-level vision. One interesting outcome of the discussions in the United States was the addition of an initiative focused on K–12 education. Simply put, many of our alumni, while championing the global perspective, urged us to take on what they saw as the biggest U.S. societal problem. They were right, so we made the addition to our original plan.

Unfortunately, the K–12 initiative did not have the benefit of a long academic planning process. As a result, it never achieved the broad engagement of multiple schools, and while it made some important contributions, it did not see the same long-term success that our other initiatives did. For me, the lesson was that one couldn't rush the gestation process for a major initiative: as clear as the need was, the process of building consensus and broad leadership across an institution takes time.

We now had a plan that had broad internal support, had been refined by a group of trustees, and had gotten the support of the board as well as a broader set of advisors. It was ready for the public to see. Any strategic plan eventually needs to be taken to the constituents: customers for a corporation, alumni and donors for a nonprofit. Do they see the plan as innovative, as far reaching, as compelling?

To communicate our vision for Stanford's future, we traveled to nineteen cities in the United States, Europe, and Asia over three years, giving more than a hundred seminars with dozens of faculty, engaging more than ten thousand alumni. I remember talking to one of our distinguished alumni after an outreach event. He told me how much his Stanford years meant to him and how he treasured them, but after what he had heard that day, he was prouder than ever to be associated with Stanford. Mission accomplished.

8

INTELLECTUAL CURIOSITY

Why Being a Lifelong Learner Is Crucial

"The important thing is not to stop questioning;
never lose a holy curiosity."
Albert Einstein

It has been said by those close to the Oval Office that once a person is elected president, learning ends. The job is so demanding, and so insulated, that it is almost impossible to learn anything new, which may be true for that unique position. Some may think the same is true for anyone who steps up to lead a large organization. Certainly it seems true for certain leaders, including some corporate CEOs and perhaps even a few university presidents.

I don't buy it.

I believe you can learn—in fact, that you should learn—at the top, pursuing subjects directly relevant to your role and your field, as well as topics of general interest that will make you a well-rounded and better-informed human being.

Of course, once you accept a leadership position, likely you will no longer have time to master any particular field of knowledge. At best you might become an informed amateur. If, on your way to leadership, you mastered a field after years of training, you might find this amateurishness frustrating. Best to accept your circumstances. Your profession is now leadership. Beyond studying to enhance your leadership skills, you should focus on informing yourself about any new or rapidly changing fields that might represent growth areas for or make an impact on your organization, such as stem cells, artificial intelligence, or neuroscience. Your goal is to learn enough to ask intelligent questions of people in these fields, to understand how they might shape your worldview or your institutional view.

This advice holds true in both university and industry settings. For example, I sit on the board of directors of Alphabet/Google. Looking at the artificial intelligence and machine learning revolution—and asking questions of colleagues at Google and Stanford—I was able to appreciate that we were about to see a discontinuity and a grand leap forward in this technology. The AlphaGo victory over world champion Go player Lee Sedol only confirmed that leap. I am by no means a master of AI technology, but because I had some background, I asked a few key questions, I listened to the questions of others, and I was able to contribute to a board-level discussion that endorsed an AI-first strategy, entailing a significant increase in Google's spending and focus on AI.

In the university setting, learning about new technology was necessary to making informed decisions about major investments. For example, one of my colleagues had invented a technique called optogenetics, which used optics both to sense and to change the state of neurons in the brain. When I saw this bold technology, I knew it would change the way we conduct neuroscience research, and in the future it could lead to new treatments for various diseases of the brain.

I admit that I wanted to learn about this technology primarily because I am an innately curious person, but my understanding of optogenetics motivated the provost and me to make a major investment in the area. I didn't need—and I certainly didn't have the time—to become an expert on the topic to discern its great potential. I simply needed to ask some questions, after which I could tell you, in layman's terms, how the technology works, including its ingenious use of a gene from a primitive alga, and why it was an important development.

For a corporate executive, this kind of eclecticism is helpful; for a university president, it is absolutely vital. Over the course of a single day, you've got to be able to talk to one colleague who's working on school reform, and recognize the pertinent issues. Then you've got to talk to someone who's working on corporate governance, and have some familiarity with the issues around compensation and board makeup. Next you need to talk with researchers from the medical school about new immunotherapy treatments for cancer. Then you meet with people from the engineering school to find out what's happening in the realm of new battery technologies. At each stop, you need to be able to understand enough argot, to ask relevant questions, and to discern how new developments may have an impact on the university.

Clearly, if you want to lead well, your learning must continue.

The Gift of Reading

I suppose I've always had a healthy dose of intellectual curiosity. As a kid, I'd happily spend hours reading the encyclopedia. When I was a young boy in the 1950s, my father, an aerospace engineer, often worked night shifts. On those evenings, my mother would usually read to us, and over the years we read most of Frank Baum's Oz stories. Her love of reading was one of her greatest gifts to me, but I didn't realize that yet.

A decade later when I headed to college, I was not terribly interested in the social events, parties, and various antics that often seem to occupy the time of many first-year students, including most of my dorm mates. I was much more focused on feeding my intellectual curiosity.

Although I did not make many friends, I did well in my classes the first semester, and persuaded the academic dean that I should be allowed to take a course overload in the spring semester. A few weeks into the spring semester, I received my monthly care package from my mom, but the usual letter was not included, just a short note saying she was having a vision problem, but not to worry, she would write soon. A month later, I received a call from my dad telling me to come home quickly because my mother was dying of cancer. My dad picked me up at the train station that evening and told me that my mom would probably die in the next few days; that night, as we talked, the call came from the hospital that my mom was gone. Our family of six kids was devastated.

I went back to school after about a week, but I had a hard time focusing—my studies were no longer compelling, and I had no one to support me emotionally. I didn't perform well that semester, and I was happy to go home when June came.

How did my family and I survive that tragedy? My mother's mom, a thoughtful, patient, and gentle soul, gave up her own life and came to live with my family on and off for the next several years, playing a key role in the care of my younger siblings. For me, being back with my family and friends enabled me to regain my balance. Although my mom was gone, I came to realize how much she had given me—my love of reading, my desire to learn ever more about the world—and how I could use those gifts on the road ahead. In essence, my mom has remained with me every step along the way, and I have tried to live my life in a way that would make her proud.

Learning from Others' Experiences

I continue to be a voracious reader today, because learning makes life more interesting. In his book about Leonardo da Vinci, Walter Isaacson notes that da Vinci documented his curiosity across 7,200 notebook pages—a clear mark of a person who enjoyed the pursuit of knowledge and deep exploration of the possible. I suspect we share a similar insatiable desire to learn. Beyond personal enjoyment, though, this lifelong curiosity has served me well in my career. It has enabled me to engage in meaningful dialog about the world and its future.

When my leadership responsibilities expanded from the relatively homogeneous School of Engineering to the wildly heterogeneous university, suddenly I was deeply conscious of how much I didn't know. Across Stanford's roughly one hundred departments and programs, there were many disciplines about which I knew less than an undergraduate studying in that field.

Immediately, I doubled down on my reading, and I explored a few fields that seemed critical and in which I had little knowledge. As a scientist, one of my biggest challenges was learning about the core humanities. While my wife of forty-plus years—an artist from a family of artists—had educated me about the visual arts, and my love of fiction had exposed me to some literary traditions, I still had work to do. I began reading the *New York Review of Books*, which focuses on important books in the literary and historical sectors. Many of these books were more scholarly than what I would typically choose, but they proved valuable in preparing me for the task ahead.

Most important, though, I focused on reading about my new leadership role. I'd been a long-time student of Lincoln, but now I branched out, trying to understand what made leaders such as Teddy Roosevelt, Lyndon Johnson, and others great. Johnson especially interested me. Though his legacy is besmirched by Vietnam, he has one of the finest records when it comes to domestic programs (perhaps second only to FDR in modern times). I wanted to understand how Johnson did that, and I found compelling answers to that in Robert Caro's book *Master of the Senate*.

I'd always loved reading histories and biographies to understand the trajectory of great cities, countries, and civilizations. Now I focused my reading on questions of leadership, historical breakthroughs, and historical disasters (especially those that were avoidable). I read the stories of great leaders to examine their habits, to understand what characteristics helped make them successful, to see how they prepared themselves for moments of crisis, and to understand how they handled success and—perhaps more important—failure.[1]

Since I had few peers to talk to about leadership issues, I found comfort and support in having "conversations" with these figures of the past, who had faced challenges far greater than my own and survived (this too, I found comforting). Obviously, the problems of, say, 1785 had to be translated to the twenty-first century, but I was pleasantly surprised how much the human element retained a consistency—in motivation, action, and decision making—across centuries.

For example, what made George Washington, against all odds, so successful in leading an army of undersupplied and undertrained men to defeat their better-prepared British counterparts? I learned that Washington's leadership characteristics were critical, as were his strategies.

In the British system, the officers were gentlemen and the enlisted men were not—a class system that reflected British life. As a wealthy landowner himself, Washington could have structured his army similarly. Instead, he chose to treat the enlisted men in the Continental Army as his colleagues, not as subservient individuals.[2] Of course, he remained in charge and he gave the orders—everybody understood that, but did he treat these soldiers as though they didn't belong? Did he refuse to be seated at the same table with them? No, and that's why those citizen soldiers fought for him with near unfathomable loyalty.

Literature, biographies, and histories—they're like laboratories in which we can examine and learn critical lessons without having to live the difficulties ourselves. Reading about failures helped me understand both how to avoid some mistakes and how to recover from others. I learned that the best leaders don't just accept failure, they take responsibility for it, and they fight to turn failure into success.

Washington almost lost the war on Long Island and Manhattan, but he came back. Lincoln stuck with McClellan for far too long before replacing him—he had to learn, only after many opportunities to end the war early were missed, to become a commander-in-chief.

Kennedy endured the Bay of Pigs; Johnson wrestled with Vietnam. Some leaders recovered from their failures; others did not. I learned from examining each of them.

It's easy to accept the laurels for success, though ideally you will recognize that the people who worked for you deserve those laurels as much as, if not more than, you do. It's not so easy to admit that you were wrong and accept responsibility for your mistakes. This is where many leaders go astray: they blame failures on their subordinates. Not only is it morally wrong to blame others but, practically speaking, doing so will destroy your credibility as a leader.

In challenging moments, great leaders show their true character. Grant admitted that the final, disastrous charge at Cold Harbor was the greatest mistake of his life, one that cost thousands of lives, and Ike, in advance, wrote a letter accepting blame for the (potential) failure of the Normandy Invasion. Their stories taught me if you can't take the blame for failure, you shouldn't take the job.

I also learned from my reading that great leaders don't make the same mistake twice. More than that, when they encounter a similar situation again, they have already thought long and hard about the previous failure, and they have already formulated a new strategy for success. Leaders analyze their failures from every angle, until they know it better than many people know their successes. This is not about guilt or self-recrimination; it is about learning to do better the next time. In these leaders' analyses of their failures, I recognized a pattern: they took a scientifically curious, empirical approach. What went wrong? What can be changed? How can you move further along the learning curve to success? All leaders—not just presidents and military officers, but also scientists, CEOs, and entrepreneurs—need to face failure with humility, courage, and intelligence.

I once asked Walter Isaacson why he was driven to include the shortcomings of various leaders he wrote about, including Albert Einstein, Steve Jobs, and Benjamin Franklin. He said, "I wanted to show that individuals can be very successful despite their shortcomings and failures." Yes, we all have character flaws, and we all make mistakes. What matters is that you avoid mistakes when you can, accept and recover from them when they come, and then move on.

I encountered my own failure in the New York City campus deal (see Chapter 5, "Courage"). I extricated Stanford from the deal before my desire for successful resolution outweighed the reality of the situation. I also failed in my first attempt at expanding the undergraduate enrollment (see Chapter 6, "Collaboration and Teamwork"). In that case, I realized I had failed to make a compelling argument in favor of expansion. I learned my lesson, and we came back with a wholly different approach the next time around.

Having explored the successes and failures of great leaders, I understood these failures in a larger context. I did not personalize them. Rather I saw failure as part of the leadership journey, and therefore I recovered quickly.

I've used my mistakes to teach others as well. When telling the story of MIPS to my students, I make it a point to share the biggest mistake I made as an inexperienced entrepreneur. While our vision of the technology succeeded, we founders, three young PhDs with virtually no business experience, failed to maintain adequate decision-making power—we gave up a dedicated founder seat on the board of directors. As a result, the board made important decisions without our input. The decisions didn't kill the company, but they slowed its trajectory and they increased—by perhaps $20 million—the money we needed to bring the company to its IPO. That's my greatest regret—our mistake meant more ownership dilution, taking money out of the pockets of the employees who had worked hard to make the company a success. None of us founders ever made that mistake again. I share that story often, hoping others will learn to avoid such a mistake themselves.

Ultimately, no matter what your industry, field of study, or leadership position, you can prepare yourself for success—and for failure—by staying curious and learning from others.

My Library

I am convinced that my lifelong habit of reading—especially reading stories of successful leaders—shaped my tenure as Stanford president. That same belief in the power of great histories and biographies will inform the curriculum of the Knight-Hennessy Scholars. If our scholars are destined to lead the future, then what better preparation than to learn from the leaders of the past?

In the Coda, you'll find a list of books that have helped me in my own education in leadership, consoled me during tough times, and given me perspective during good times. It includes biographies of political leaders, books about innovations and scientific discoveries, and books about U.S. and world history. I share these titles with humility, knowing that what worked for me may not work for you. At least I hope this list inspires you to create a similar library of your own.

You'll notice the list focuses on nonfiction, but I am also an avid consumer of fiction, so at the end I share some of my favorite fiction writers.

9

STORYTELLING

Communicating a Vision

"No, no! The adventures first, explanations take such a dreadful time."
Lewis Carroll, Alice's Adventures in Wonderland

Let me tell you a story. . .

That's how I began a talk I gave to Stanford's trustees, at a retreat in Pebble Beach, California. We were enjoying dinner together at a small house overlooking the ocean at Point Joe, on 17-Mile Drive. The latest news about the university was good, and everyone was in great spirits.

I was nearing the end of my presidency, and I had been wondering if there was one last "big thing" I'd like to accomplish, as a capstone. An idea had percolated in my mind over the previous few months. I'd tested it out with several university leaders and the chair of the board, Steve Denning. Now I would try the idea out with the trustees. I knew I was taking a risk, and I knew that the best way to introduce a new idea is not with facts and figures, but with a story.

So I began, "One hundred fifteen years ago, a prominent British businessman started a scholarship program for promising young people around the world. Over time, this program has become so successful that most people, who otherwise would never have heard Cecil Rhodes's name, know of the Rhodes Foundation and the Rhodes Scholars. His investment in turning outstanding students into world-class leaders has produced enormous returns over the years.

Just listen to the names of some of the scholars who came out of that program," and I mentioned a few—Mike McFaul, ambassador to Russia; Cory Booker and Bill Bradley, U.S. Senators; James Woolsey, CIA director; Susan Rice, national security advisor; Michael Spence, Nobel Prize winner and former dean of Stanford School of Business; David Frohmayer, former president of the University of Oregon; and authors Walter Isaacson, former president of Aspen Institute; Atul Gawande, Harvard Medical School; and Siddhartha Mukherjee, Columbia Medical School. It's a remarkable legacy.

Having captured the trustees' attention, I continued, "You know, we at Stanford should try to create a similar kind of program for the twenty-first century. Open to women, not just men. Open to people of color, not just white men. Open to the entire world, not just primarily former British colonies." The Rhodes program had made these changes over time, but Stanford would have the benefit of starting anew, in the twenty-first century, not at the end of the nineteenth.

For final consideration, I offered my audience this vision: "Given Stanford's West Coast location, diversity, academic quality, and entrepreneurial culture—just think of the class of leaders a program like this could help create twenty or thirty years down the road." Then I placed the trustees in my vision. "Think of how proud we will feel, having established such a program and invested in its future."

My risk paid off. The trustees responded with enthusiasm, and I knew exactly who I wanted to talk to next: Phil Knight, founder of Nike and a legendary philanthropist.

I knew Phil was as concerned about leadership as I was, not just in government but in all parts of modern society. I knew he was concerned that many contemporary leaders were making unwise decisions. Why? I'd say they didn't necessarily have the knowledge, relevant experience, or the right values. Finally, I knew Phil still believed in the power of innovation and entrepreneurial thinking, so I had good reason to believe he would be interested in an initiative that focused on preparing creative thinkers to engage in transformative leadership.

When I flew up to Oregon to meet with Phil, the cornerstone of the conversation would be my story about the Rhodes program, but I wanted to lay some groundwork first. So I told Phil something he already knew: we've got a giant leadership problem, not just in government, but also in the corporate world (witness Volkswagen and Wells Fargo) and in the nonprofit world (witness the raft of NCAA athletics scandals). I talked about what Rhodes had done more than a century earlier and then turned to the future. I described how a highly selective leadership program, drawing talent from around the globe to Stanford and its entrepreneurial culture—a program that included students in all disciplines and encouraged the development of cross-disciplinary thinking and collaboration—could make a real difference. "If we do it well enough," I said, "and if we're careful enough, and if we measure ourselves and hold ourselves accountable, it'll have great outcomes."

Phil replied, "Give me some time to think about it."

No one says yes to an initiative of this magnitude overnight. An idea like this has to inhabit one's imagination for a while. Phil needed to live with it for a bit before he would know if the project was right for him. Meanwhile, I returned to my duties at Stanford.

About a month later, I got the call: "I'm ready to talk about it," Phil said.

I told him that we'd fly up to Portland to meet him. "No," he said, "I'm coming down to you." It was an unforgettable meeting, because Phil got right to the point: he would commit to a $400 million gift on two conditions: first, he asked that I share the billing with him; second, he asked me to act as the program's inaugural director. "If we can agree on that," he said, "then we can do it."

I took his conditions as a compliment, and I've worked with enough business leaders to know these conditions carried a deeper motive: Phil wanted to know whether I was fully committed, or simply involved. What's the difference? Think of a traditional bacon and egg breakfast: the chicken is involved, but the pig is committed.

As I retired from the presidency, at a stage in life when some people are booking travel reservations and scheduling tee times, was I ready to devote my time and energy to building the Knight-Hennessy Scholars program into a thriving institution, even if it took years? Yes, I was.

Note that this chain of events began with telling a story. Indeed, the first trustee I consulted, Steve Denning, became one of the most important advocates for the Knight-Hennessy Scholars. In addition to helping solicit other gifts for the program's endowment, Steve and Roberta Denning gave a gift to create Denning House, the inspiring home for the Knight-Hennessy Scholars.

Engaging the Heart

So many great endeavors—from social movements to tech innovations—begin with stories. We like to think we are rational creatures—that all we need to do is deliver a quantitative evaluation of a concept, idea, or program, and logic will prevail—but the truth lies elsewhere.

Sure, facts and figures can capture our brains, but they aren't very good at capturing our hearts. We may agree with a proposal—or at least go along with it—because the logic seems impeccable, but does the logic energize us? Rarely. On the other hand, when a meme or movement thrills us, engages us, or makes us feel valuable, we jump on board, logic be damned.

For this reason, if you really want to inspire a team to action, best to engage them with a story. Once they become receptive—once they can imagine themselves as part of your vision—you can back your story up with facts and figures.

Of course, when you're leading your team in a new direction, you may not have any facts and figures. All you have is a plan. Whether you're building a novel product, creating a new educational mechanism, or initiating a research program, you simply don't have quantitative data to share.

You do, however, have a dream. When you turn that dream into a vivid story, you make it so attractive and so real that people will want to share it with you by joining your team. They know that failure is a real possibility, that they will have to work hard with little reward (at least at first), and that they could be doing easier work elsewhere, but they want to be part of the movement. They want to be part of something bigger and more important than their individual selves, and, if they trust you, they will follow you into new territory.[1]

No one ever enlisted anyone into that kind of effort with a pie chart and some PowerPoint slides. Rather, you need to be able to capture people's hearts and imaginations. You need to share your vision, irresistibly.

Crafting the Vision as a Story

When I was collaborating with my Stanford colleagues to develop a strategic plan for the university (see Chapter 7, "Innovation"), we identified a central theme: multidisciplinary research and teaching focused on important world problems. The plan would form the basis for a major fundraising campaign, the Stanford Challenge. To convince potential supporters that we could accomplish the mission set out in our plan, we needed a story. We had to show them that we could work together in multidisciplinary teams, not something academics are known for, and that we could apply that talent to solving important, practical problems. Fortunately, Bio-X, which Jim Clark had supported, served as a prototype for such interdisciplinary work and provided us with a great story.

As part of establishing Bio-X and deploying Clark's gift, we had established a "seed venture fund" that provided early-stage research support for novel collaborations among faculty members from different disciplines, who were working together for the first time. One early proposal came from colleagues in chemical engineering and ophthalmology, who wanted to develop an artificial cornea. In the West, corneal transplants are done using material from cadavers, but this solution does not work well in less-developed parts of the world, and in war-torn countries where the number of ocular injuries, including to U.S. soldiers, exceeds the availability of donors.

This interdisciplinary team came up with a novel solution, obtained significant follow-on funding, and began transplants in animals as a prelude to human deployment. They had shown that cross-disciplinary collaboration could achieve something remarkable: giving sight back to an injured person. This story became a part of our outreach events as we engaged supporters in the Stanford Challenge.

Stanford University's history is full of rich stories, such as the founding of the university by a California railway tycoon and his wife mourning the death of their son; the 1906 earthquake; and our unequalled sporting achievements, earning at least one NCAA championship for forty-two years in a row. Many of the university's most celebrated stories, though, relate to Silicon Valley, which found its roots at Stanford.

Fred Terman, the son of a Stanford professor, and a professor himself, started one of the first electronics programs west of the Mississippi, in the early 1930s. To his lab, located in a set of outbuildings behind the Stanford Quad, he drew some of the best electrical engineering minds in America. Generations of engineers, solid-state physicists, and, later, computer scientists came, and they in turn branched out into the surrounding communities, including Stanford Industrial Park (also founded by Terman), creating the digital revolution. Today the world's leading venture capital community also abuts the Stanford campus—no coincidence there.

From these events, hundreds of stories have arisen. Each year, I see new freshmen arrive and, like pilgrims to holy shrines, visit the places on campus where Hewlett and Packard experimented, where the Varian Brothers built the klystron tube (radar), where Jerry Yang and Dave Filo helped devise Yahoo!, and where Sergey Brin and Larry Page started Google. Because they know these stories, many students come to Stanford to emulate these now iconic entrepreneurs. To paraphrase the musical *Hamilton*, they want to be on the campus where it happened.

These stories continue to live in the imaginations of each new generation of inventors and entrepreneurs, and they guided our vision when we began thinking about developing a new science and engineering quadrangle. My primary goal was to build on the success of Bio-X and the Clark building, to create four new multidisciplinary engineering and science buildings, housing forward-thinking activities, from nanoscience to bioengineering, to environmental science and engineering, to our program in entrepreneurship. I hoped that we could find donors who would be inspired by this vision and, more specifically, that we could find donors who were entrepreneurs to name the four buildings.

Happily, we achieved our goals: those four buildings house faculty members from about ten departments and programs, and they include space for student collaboration and project fabrication. Further, they reflect our storied history. In the basement of the building housing the headquarters of the School of Engineering is a replica of the very small garage where Hewlett-Packard began, including a lab bench containing their first product. The four donors to the buildings, Jensen Huang (founder of NVidia), Jim Spilker (founder of Stanford Telecommunications), Jerry Yang (founder of Yahoo), and Ram Shriram (founding board member of Google), are all successful Stanford-connected entrepreneurs. When prospective and current students walk through this quadrangle, they hear the stories of a new generation of innovators who built on the legacy established long ago by Hewlett and Packard. Hence our stories continue to attract and inspire the next great entrepreneurial minds.

Of course, not all these attempts were a success. For example, I failed to find a donor for a new science building, despite several promising leads. In such cases, we had to make hard choices, since deciding to go ahead with the building would mean taking on additional debt and thirty years of debt payments. In such cases, I realized that I was letting down my colleagues who would either have to forgo their new facility or live with the budgetary limitations imposed by the debt payments.

Stories Work in the Business World as Well

In their book *Built to Last*, Jim Collins and Jerry Porras opened people's eyes to the power of business storytelling. In their research, which involved nineteen companies noted for their enduring success and consistent innovation, Collins and Porras discovered each was rich in company myths and legends. These stories—such as David Packard giving an award to a product manager who rightly ignored Packard's order to abandon a new product initiative—gave companies a sense of continuity, uniqueness, and common cause, and they helped assimilate new employees into the company culture. The authors found that when it came time to respond to change, these companies moved quickly and efficiently, because every employee already understood the company identity and therefore knew how to respond without direct coaching.

Stories play an important role in entrepreneurial start-ups as well. After all, what are start-ups but enterprises trying to convince investors, potential employees, and future customers to buy in to their stories? Typically, a start-up team doesn't have a product yet, and sometimes the products they propose (such as a social network or a phone app) will never take on a material form. So all the founders have is a dream of what could be. What enables them to convey this dream to potential stakeholders? Stories. The company that tells the richest and most believable story—backed up by a business plan that is itself a story—procures the funding to make that dream come true.

It may sound like I'm overstating the case—that stories can't possibly have this much power. In my experience, though, dreams are often self-fulfilling. If enough people buy into a dream, it becomes reality. Steve Jobs said he was going to give us affordable personal computers (then handheld jukeboxes, electronic tablets, and smart cell phones). We believed, and he delivered—each time, making enough money to fund the next dream. Larry Page and Sergey Brin aimed to "Organize the world's information and make it universally accessible and useful." Elon Musk was going to give us practical electric cars. We believed, and they delivered.

I believe that in every profession and career, as we climb to higher leadership positions, the role of facts and data decreases. Sure, facts form a set of boundaries that we must account for, but our task is to find solutions to complex problems, despite limitations imposed by facts and figures. We find ourselves increasingly concerned with seeking new possibilities and with creating visions of how those possibilities could be realized. Yes, facts and data still determine the structure of what we do, but they cannot formulate a vision.

When you move from the field in which you built your career—scientific research, marketing, sales, or what have you—and step into leadership, your technical talent will become less important and data will become just another tool. Now you must develop your ability to bring people together, to inspire them, to mentor them, and to lead them in the direction of your vision. In this phase of your career, one of your most powerful skills, you will find, is an ability to tell appropriate, compelling, and inspiring stories.

Collecting the Stories

Where do these stories come from? I don't have any easy answer to that. If you are part of a long-established institution, it's likely institutional history will offer up a vast inventory of stories—indeed, perhaps one appropriate for almost any occasion.

A start-up or young company can draw upon stories from other institutions. In Silicon Valley, numerous companies, including Apple, borrowed Hewlett-Packard stories at their beginnings. Semiconductor companies regularly tell stories about Intel's founders: driven CEO Andy Grove, cerebral Gordon Moore, and inspiring Bob Noyce. Many notable recent start-ups—including Tesla and LinkedIn

—took their stories from their personal histories, their founders' days at PayPal. Meanwhile, history books contain endless numbers of usable stories. So, in fact, do your competitors. For example, even with all of the great Stanford stories, I love to tell a story that comes from a minister at Harvard.

Peter Gomes, the Pusey Minister at Harvard's Memorial Church for many years, was giving the baccalaureate talk at the beginning of graduation weekend at Stanford. Getting up to give advice to our graduating students, he said, "Your whole object here is not to make a living but it is to make a life that is worth living." Then, looking out at the students sitting before him, with their parents sitting behind them, he quoted a former Harvard president, A. Lawrence Lowell, who said, "True success does not consist in doing what we set forth to do, what we had hoped to do, nor even in doing what we have struggled to do, but in doing something that is worth doing." I watched his message sail right over that sea of twenty-two-year-olds and land with their parents, who nodded in response—they'd seen enough of life to understand the truth of his statement. Most of the students, however, as smart as they were, were just too young to get it.

As you might imagine, I have told that story to a number of Stanford alumni who were considering becoming donors to the university. Certainly they already had personal connections to Stanford as their alma mater, but often that wasn't enough to elicit a donation. After all, people with their means are often being pulled in multiple directions to invest money—on personal expenditures, business investments, and charitable donations. Why then should they give to Stanford, with its already extravagant endowment?

I'm happy to show them charts and graphs, awards and lists of achievements, but at most such things reinforce what these individuals already know: Stanford is one of the world's great universities. In the end, their decisions come down to stories. For example, when trying to raise money for student scholarships, we would invite current students to tell their stories about being accepted to a university that, twenty years before, they would never have dreamed of attending because their families were too poor, or no family member had ever attended college, or they grew up in a single-parent home. At a presentation about undergraduate financial aid, one of our trustees was the storyteller. She described growing up in Chicago, the daughter of a housekeeper, stuffing plastic bags in the bottoms of her shoes before she walked to school because the soles had holes in them. That story, told by such a distinguished and accomplished individual, says more about the transformative effect of higher education than any number of charts.

In collecting stories, you are taking the raw material of daily campus life and finding the transformative image within—whether it's a homeless young woman coming to Stanford or it's some new visionary research and its potential applications. When you listen, you'll find that these stories present themselves to you, often multiple times a day.

I received a gem of a story when, early in my presidency, Itzhak Perlman came to Stanford to give a violin recital. In the green room of Memorial Auditorium, which was, as the name says, an auditorium, not a music venue, Mr. Perlman greeted me, saying, "Mr. President, Stanford is a great university, but it has terrible performance facilities!"

He was right, and I repeated that story frequently as we tried to gain momentum for Stanford's ambitious arts initiative. At one point, Peter Bing, one of Stanford's longest-serving trustees and a former board chair, stepped forward to be the lead donor on a new concert hall. Peter not only provided the naming gift for the Bing Concert Hall but also devoted considerable time to ensuring that the Hall would be acoustically and aesthetically outstanding, as well as comfortable. When the financial crisis hit in 2008, and it appeared that we might have to delay or cancel the concert hall, a number of trustees who believed in the arts and were moved by Peter's focus on excellence in the design stepped forward to help us complete the project. Today, the Bing Concert Hall is one of the finest medium-scale concert halls on any campus.

Of course, retelling old stories has its weaknesses: many people have already heard them, and the stories themselves can go stale, losing their purchase on a changing world. That's why it's important to look and listen, perpetually, for new stories.

In the academic world, the campus press office and alumni magazine are excellent sources for timely and relatively unheard stories. Even more effective, though, is a simple walk around campus. Get out of the office, talk to students, chat with faculty members—one is bound to pick up good stories. In the corporate world, the company newsletter, website, and magazine are valuable sources. So are trade shows and other industry gatherings, but as in the academy, some of the best stories are picked up in casual settings with employees.

Of course, you don't need to rush off and assiduously write down every story you hear. Rather, you need to develop an "ear" for the telling anecdote, the wise lesson, and the illuminating story. Jot down some notes when you get the chance, or just remember who told it to you so you can get back to them for details. As a university president or corporate CEO, your goal is to have a regularly refreshed quiver full of stories you can pull out for almost any occasion, especially when you are asked to speak extemporaneously.

Meanwhile, practice your storytelling skills for those times when you need to sell your audience on your vision of something that does not yet exist. Fill that story with as much verisimilitude as possible—make your audience live it—and you just may enlist them to help you change the world.

The Knight-Hennessy Scholars program will accept its first class in 2018, about the time this book is published. As I write this, we are reviewing over 3,600 applications for the first fifty slots. Remember—this project, like so many other life-changing endeavors, began with a story.

10

LEGACY

What You Leave Behind

"The great use of a life is to spend it for something that outlasts it."
Attributed to William James

I remember the first time someone asked me about my legacy. It happened in the summer of 2015, shortly after I had announced my intention to resign at the end of the next academic year. The question arose in discussions about farewell events and articles that would celebrate our achievements over the past sixteen years.

To tell you the truth, I never thought in terms of legacy, neither during my sixteen years as president nor in my earlier leadership roles. Instead, I thought about leading authentically and ethically, to build trust with the Stanford community so that together we could improve Stanford in ways that would last far beyond my leadership.

To achieve this collective goal, we needed to emphasize and invest in the right initiatives. Hence, we focused on building the endowment for financial aid, so future generations would have access to more financial assistance. Similarly, in choosing where to expand our multidisciplinary efforts, we targeted areas—such as environmental sustainability, international affairs, and human health—in which we expected major challenges not just in the next decade but fifty years in the future.

In short, I hadn't thought much about what I would leave behind; I'd been too busy building what I hoped would last long into the future. So when people asked me about my legacy back in 2015, I was somewhat hesitant to answer. "Be humble and let others sing your praises"—that was my instinct. In all honesty, I was as likely to think about what we hadn't gotten done yet as about what we had accomplished.

Focusing on What Matters

I suppose one could start thinking about legacy on the first day of one's career. Certainly, being conscious of the long-term implications of one's actions and decisions could produce salutary effects. At the very least, it could serve as a check on immoral actions. Then again, one's scruples should be enough to keep one on the straight path ethically. More likely, an overemphasis on legacy could limit one's career and tarnish one's reputation. For example, a person obsessed with the final scoreboard is prone to risk-aversion, as in the case of General McClellan, who, despite his popularity with the troops, was removed by Lincoln because he was afraid to risk losing a battle. In fact, he did his best to avoid battles. Further, a person who wishes to build a legacy of altruism may do the exact opposite if his actions come not from a deep concern for others' well-being but from a desire to project a certain image. A leader with a dedicated, lifelong habit of service builds a legacy; a leader who merely appears for photo ops creates a reputation of inauthenticity.

Rather than legacy-building, the early years of your career should be devoted to doing the best job you can in your chosen profession—building your skills, gaining experience, and establishing yourself as an individual and a team member. No one knows what opportunities may follow from there. In my case, in my early days as an engineering student, I simply wanted to become a computer engineer. When I became a professor, I was never happier. When an entrepreneurial opportunity arose, I took it. Then I became a dean, and I realized that I had an aptitude for leadership, which led to my becoming provost and then president. Now, in my sixties, I've assumed a new role, directing the Knight-Hennessy Scholars program.

What if, at twenty-five, forty, or fifty years old, I had been busy shepherding my reputation and avoiding risks? I would have missed my opportunity to found a start-up in Silicon Valley. I would have turned down the job of provost. Today I would be resting on the reputation I built as president of Stanford, not launching a brand-new venture. Instead of worrying about my legacy too much or too early, I'm choosing now—as I always have—to follow the path of making meaningful contributions. Focusing my life's work on making a difference seems a far better strategy than being either a young person obsessing about my image or an old person trying to burnish a mediocre or damaged reputation in my final years.

Often what guided my behavior was not legacy-building, but guarding my limited time, energy, and resources. I think of this as the opportunity cost dilemma. The opportunity cost is your time, your energy, and your stature—your ability to use your position to do something that matters. To do the greatest good, you need regularly to ask yourself, How can I use my time and my position most effectively?

Of course, when you're in a top leadership position, you carry tremendous responsibility, with many factors operating outside your control. If a scandal erupts, if a major initiative fails, you likely will need to take responsibility. Fear of such disruptions could paralyze a leader, so you need to stay focused on moving forward: How can you improve your organization? How can you lead your institution in a direction that will set it apart and make a positive impact on the world?

In my case, the Stanford Challenge set that direction—a capital campaign aimed at transforming both research and teaching to support multidisciplinary initiatives focused on major global challenges. The Challenge took a decade to plan and execute, and it focused my attention on what really mattered: leaving the university better than it was when I started.

To my mind, legacy means ensuring that others have benefitted from your work. If you're leading an institution, legacy means the institution you serve becomes better in some concrete, clearly defined way under your service. It means the institution serves people more effectively now than it did when you arrived. This definition of legacy applies to all types of organizations, and all individuals within them, at all levels of leadership.

Your Role Shapes Your Legacy

At any point in time, your role in your organization will largely define the scope of your legacy. If you're a faculty member, your legacy is, in part, your research, at least to the extent that it makes an impact on the world or other scholars. The heart of your legacy, however, is the students you graduate. That's why, in the academic world, we talk about academic "children" and "grandchildren"—the generation of students we've educated and, among those who have gone on to be professors, their students.

This legacy is reflected in a celebration we host in the academic world, often called a Festschrift, when a professor is nearing retirement. Typically this event includes a series of seminars, sometimes a whole-day conference, and a dinner. The high point of the celebration comes when former students and colleagues talk about the professor's research or about how their own work has been shaped by the professor's mentorship.

At Stanford, we also honor the legacy of high school teachers who have helped develop our students, with the Frederick Emmons Terman Engineering Scholastic Award. Every year, the School of Engineering celebrates the top 5 percent of the senior class that's about to graduate. The awardees get to invite their most influential high school teachers to this event, at Stanford's expense. I have participated a half-dozen times, both as a faculty advisor to an awardee and as the dean, and it is one of the most moving events I have witnessed. One time, a teacher who attended showed me a picture from her school. She had posted our invitation letter on the bulletin board in the faculty lunchroom. She was proud to tell people, not only did this student choose me, but Stanford is paying for me to go.

When these teachers are asked to speak about their students, they humbly share how they knew these students were special, taking no credit for the students' achievements, while the students talk about how the teachers inspired them. Tellingly, these teachers represent all disciplines. Predictably, we see physics, computer science, and math teachers, but we also see foreign language teachers (often Latin), English teachers, or debate coaches in the mix—a reminder that even in STEM disciplines, humanities teachers have great influence.

The event sends a message to those teachers who made a difference: here's your legacy; the student you helped inspire is going on to do great things. In fact, the award is named for and was funded by a legendary professor, dean, and provost, who donated the royalties from his textbooks to the university to create this remarkable tradition.

Of course, Stanford University itself grew from a legacy. Every year, on Founders' Day, we celebrate Leland and Jane Stanford's gift that created the university. Traditionally, we ask students to submit essays, two of which are chosen—one from an undergraduate and one from a graduate student—to be read during the day's ceremonies.

One year, our speaker was Stanford's first student from Mongolia. A graduate student in International Policy Studies, she was investigating how democracies are built, an understanding she intended to bring back to Mongolia, to work toward democracy there. After taking the podium, she related a little of her history, and then said, "I'm standing here, wondering, what if Jane and Leland Stanford were sitting in the audience? What would they say? Could they ever have imagined that there'd be a woman from a country halfway around the world, coming to their university to study with the ambition of building a democracy in her country?" That student reminded us all: our legacy is the long-term reach of the actions we take, which can extend far beyond our imaginations.

Shaping Your Legacy over Time

When you are starting your career, you can't really know where you're going, nor can you think much about legacy. What you can think about, however, is your reputation. Take, for example, the trajectory of an academic's career. Early on, a faculty member knows the importance of publication, so she will try to publish even the smallest discovery if she thinks editors and reviewers will accept it. After establishing a credible reputation, however, she may find herself becoming more selective. At this stage of her career, she thinks, "You know what? I can probably get this published—it's got my name on it, and it meets minimal standards. However, it's not something that will enhance my reputation." This professor has realized that, for better or worse, she'll be remembered only for a limited number of achievements, so why not try to make them all excellent?

Think of a great figure such as Abraham Lincoln. He's remembered for winning the Civil War and eliminating slavery. We often forget that he signed the Homestead Act, the Morrill (Land Grant College) Act, and the Transcontinental Railroad Act—all three of which opened up the West. These fall away in our memories because of his greater achievements. This suggests that, in thinking of your legacy, you should focus on transcendent and lasting initiatives and actions.

Although we often associate these transcendent acts with the topmost leader of an organization, in fact people throughout an institution contribute as well. Edward Stanton, as Lincoln's secretary of war, and U.S. Grant, as his top general, played key parts in winning the Civil War. Charles Morrill sponsored and fought for the Morrill Act, which had been vetoed by Lincoln's predecessor. These achievements are part of their legacies as well as Lincoln's, whether or not they receive top billing in the history books.

It's hard to predict *a priori* which of our actions might have the biggest and most enduring impact: we simply do not know where our journey is going even over the one or two decades that most leaders are in office. When I started as Stanford's president, I certainly understood the importance of financial aid, but I never would have predicted that we would commit ourselves to the largest increase in undergraduate financial aid in the university's history. I also had no idea that we would launch and complete a major effort to enhance the arts at Stanford. Not only is the road ahead unpredictable, but how others will see our contributions and efforts is unpredictable. Furthermore, the interpretation of one's legacy may change over time as society changes its views of both the positive and negative aspects of one's legacy. Consider Woodrow Wilson, once praised for his leadership during World War I and his efforts to establish the League of Nations, but now condemned for his racist views. I am reminded of a line from the Gettysburg Address, "The world will little note, nor long remember what we say here." *Au contraire:* predicting the future is very hard.

Helping Others Create Their Legacies

In a sense, no matter the level of leadership at which you serve your organization, you can help people create their legacies. Just as universities offer professors and students opportunities to do legacy-worthy work, a business—and the leadership within the business—can support employees in working toward their own lasting contributions to the world.

As the president of a university, I had the unique privilege of helping alumni create legacies with longevity at Stanford. Many of our alumni who have reached great heights in their careers attribute at least part of their success to their time at Stanford. They want to acknowledge this through gifts to the university. Now, some people think that legacy means putting one's name on a building, but the alumni I worked with wanted more—they wanted to provide opportunities for the next generation of faculty and students, in a lasting way.

Why, after all their success, are these alumni interested in their legacies? Already they have achieved so much—they have run or financed major companies, gaining fortune and (for some) fame along the way. Why do they want something more? I see two motivators at work: a desire to give back, combined with an interest in establishing a legacy that lasts long into the future. In business, particularly in Silicon Valley, today's billion-dollar company—the one that puts a CEO's face on the cover of *Forbes*—may dissolve tomorrow. Certainly an individual's role as leader of a company won't last for much more than a decade or two. After peaking in their stellar careers, people often find themselves wondering, what do I want to do with my life, with my assets—my money, network, and energies? Why not make a positive change and leave the world a better place?

Does putting one's name on a building really make a difference? Well, excellent facilities enable ground-breaking research that can improve people's lives. Universities like Stanford have world-class faculties and students, but to do transformational work, particularly in the sciences and engineering, they need state-of-the-art facilities. Of course, buildings don't last forever, unless one is willing to create a fund to maintain or replace that building in perpetuity, as the Dennings have done for Denning House.

As I learned after I became president, people do care about legacy, but in rather different ways. Hewlett and Packard cared about providing excellent facilities, supporting students, and underwriting new programs. When it came to naming a building, though, they did so in honor of their teacher and mentor, Fredrick Terman Jr. Later the two buildings that frame the entrance to the science and engineering quadrangle were named for Hewlett and Packard, a request made by the university and approved by the Hewlett and Packard families, only after Bill and Dave had passed away.

Like Hewlett and Packard, some people prefer not to connect their names with their legacies. John Morgridge, former CEO of Cisco, and his wife Tashia have made major gifts to Stanford to fund buildings, professorships, and student scholarships. Yet to date no buildings on campus bear their names. Indeed, legacy doesn't have to have one's name on it. When I go to Florence, I love to get up close to the Duomo to study the intricate images engraved in the marble: a beautiful beetle, butterfly, flower, or fig leaf. Some artisan carved what must have taken hundreds of hours, without signing it. That artist's name is lost, but the work endures—a legacy appreciated more than eight hundred years later.

When I was president, as with the leader of any nonprofit, part of my job was to help financially successful people decide how to direct their philanthropy. I approached this effort with two objectives: to show them the joy of helping others, and to connect them with opportunities to make a difference consistent with what they wished to leave behind.

These efforts resulted in the Bing Concert Hall (see Chapter 9, "Storytelling") and the Anderson Collection (see Chapter 6, "Collaboration and Teamwork")—two major steps forward in our efforts to boost Stanford's position in the arts. Still, our art department itself was housed in an older building, architecturally undistinguished and short of space to accommodate the growing student demand for art studio courses. We needed donors deeply committed to the arts, and to Stanford, to help us build a building that would celebrate the importance of the visual arts.

So when I found myself on a five-hour flight to California with Burt and Deedee McMurtry, I decided I would explore their interest. They saw how a new building for the art department could become a jewel in Stanford's "arts district," the area of campus where the Cantor Art Museum, the Anderson Collection, and the Bing Concert Hall stand. They also understood how a new facility would allow students with creative interests to expand their explorations and develop their imaginations. The McMurtrys liked the proposal, and they signed on to help fund an architecturally stunning building, which Diller, Scofidio, and Renfro delivered. Today the McMurtry Art Building has become a vibrant addition to our campus and serves as a monument to the McMurtrys' joint passions for Stanford, our students, and the arts.

In my twenty years as dean, provost, and president, I attended many celebrations marking the creation of legacies through gifts of buildings, endowed chairs, and new research and education programs. In every case, at these events we reminded the donors that the faculty and students who benefited from their gifts, in this and successive generations, would be their true legacies. Those evenings always ended with smiles, hugs, and gratitude. The joy of giving was palpable, and I knew we had done our job well.

Leaving and Choosing What's Next

We all know athletes who stay too long, after their skills have deserted them and their reputations have faded. I wanted to end my presidency on a high note. In 2012, when we concluded our second fundraising campaign, I could have announced my departure. The Stanford Challenge had proven a success. We had finished the campaign on schedule, exceeding our fundraising goals by 40 percent. More important, those gifts had changed the university, growing undergraduate and graduate financial aid; transforming the engineering area of campus by replacing a set of slapdash buildings with a beautiful new quadrangle; and improving Stanford's arts offerings with a new museum, a performance venue, and studio art facilities. Further, we had created initiatives focused on major challenges facing society, such as health care; environmental sustainability; and global peace, security, and development.

By that point in my tenure, many friends and colleagues believed that I had accomplished enough, and they understood that every day I stayed on the job increased the risk that some scandal or controversy could erupt, marring my legacy. I, however, was less concerned about these risks, and more intent on making sure the transformations we had made would thrive in the long term. Some programs needed a few more years of shepherding. Meanwhile, I needed time to consider what I wanted to do next. If I had a final act at Stanford, what would it be?

When I imagined my retirement from the presidency, I did not see a clear academic direction I wanted to pursue. I thought I would do a little teaching, perhaps join a few more boards, and make some time to travel. The idea of a slower-paced life and a reduced level of responsibility had some attraction, until I had a discussion with a friend, Bill Meehan, former director at McKinsey. Bill suggested such a palette of nibbles might not satisfy me. He recommended I invest my time in one big endeavor. That endeavor became the Knight-Hennessy Scholars (see Chapter 9, "Storytelling").

My decision to step down as president and to step up as founding director of Knight-Hennessy raised a few interesting questions. First of all, if I've reached the age of retirement for the presidency, am I not too old to start up the Scholars program? When I was forty-five, I might have thought, No problem. I've got energy, I've got time, and I've got experience. At sixty-five, however, I wondered, Do I have enough energy? Will my health keep up? Do I want to re-enter start-up mode, in which everyone pitches in wherever they are needed to make the organization a success, or would I rather stick with advising roles in areas in which I've developed real expertise and can bring some hard-earned wisdom?

It's a trade-off. When you're younger, you have more energy, but with age you gain people skills, competencies, and wisdom. Just about everything you will encounter you have encountered before, and you know you will survive. Hence you will save time, money, and energy that your younger self would have wasted. Besides, there's nothing quite like the excitement of a start-up. That in itself is energizing.

Seeing Knight-Hennessy as a start-up venture raised another question: Am I willing to risk failure? Some people, the older they get, the more they guard their reputation against failures. With other people, the older they get, the less they give a damn—they are willing to pursue a promising new opportunity for its own sake. Personally, I don't worry too much about failure. I treat new endeavors as I would as a scientist. I try to assess whether something has a credible chance of success. I think about the process methodically. I ask myself, How do I test this idea? With the Knight-Hennessy Scholars, we initially tested the concept with the university's deans, then with Steve Denning, the board chair, and a few outside people, and then a larger group of people. Finally, we took it to a group of folks who might financially support us. I purposely let others contribute to the refinement of the idea—not only recognizing the value of other people's wisdom and expertise, but also giving them a stake in future success. Only then did I decide to jump in, fully committed.

I was once asked how the Bible had shaped my work as a university president. Immediately I thought of the parable of the talents (an ancient form of money). In it, three servants are given money by their employer to invest: one buries his money and is scorned by his employer on his return. The other two servants invest the funds and are rewarded. That's the point. You're given resources. You're given an opportunity. What will you do with it? If you begin with the question, How do I lead a life that makes a difference? your legacy will follow naturally from your actions.

If you really want to be remembered, do something that lasts long after you're gone. During my presidency, our team saw the development of many buildings at Stanford. That makes a positive impact, but buildings don't last forever, nor do athletic shoe companies. Phil Knight and I both understand that. We saw something in each other, and in our common vision, that could last for a very long time, empowering future generations of leaders who will leave their mark on the world. We have now convened the team that will help us do that.

Though starting such an endeavor may seem like a risk, I'm reminded—constantly—of the importance of taking such risks. For instance, during the fall of 2017, as we were reading applications for the first class of Scholars, I came across several applicants who embodied our vision. Students who had already built successful new social ventures, others dedicated to human rights or ending nuclear proliferation, or creating economic growth in the poorest parts of the world.

Phil Knight happened to be visiting that day, and as we read through a few applications, we both saw what a difference the Scholars program could make, not just in the next decade or two, but in the centuries ahead. To my mind, whether I am remembered for my contribution to that legacy is immaterial. What matters are the people who are helped along the way.

CONCLUSION

Building the Future

"How wonderful it is that no one has to wait, but can start right now
to gradually change the world!"
Anne Frank, Tales from the Secret Annex

In the fall of 2018, the inaugural cohort of scholars will begin their term at the Knight-Hennessy Scholars program. They will encounter a brand-new building administered by a brand-new staff, and brand-new opportunities for developing into transformational leaders, spearheaded by a selection of esteemed faculty members from across the university. This will mark a moment of firsts for everyone involved.

As I am writing this chapter, it is December 2017, late autumn at Stanford, or at least as autumn as the San Francisco Bay Area gets—a little rainy, the telltale leaves falling, but not cold. I have just finished teaching a freshmen seminar to some wonderful new students, and now I can feel the holiday season coming, the end of another year.

A year after stepping down from the Stanford presidency, that exciting period of my life is receding into the past. Like the bare trees on campus, already I am gearing up for rebirth—reading through scholar applications, watching construction on Denning House, and hiring the Knight-Hennessy team.

Life, as we are regularly reminded, is unpredictable. Two years ago, when I tried to imagine my life post-presidency, I pictured myself enjoying a kind of semiretirement, half corporate and half academic—the classic life of an emeritus professor or executive. Instead, while many of my peers are booking cruises or downsizing their lives, I find myself facing a completely new challenge.

When I stepped into the Stanford presidency, I assumed it would be the pinnacle of my career—a last act that would call on and grow all my skills, a chance to make a positive impact on an institution I loved. My sixteen years as president were all that and more. I never could have guessed, however, that rather than being a culmination, the presidency would become a prelude.

Leading Stanford proved the greatest challenge I had ever faced, yet I had some distinct advantages—the benefit of the institution's long history and an all-star team collaborating with me. If I succeeded, my success would be built on the triumphs of the founders and the nine presidents who had come before me. If I failed, the institution would be resilient enough to recover, albeit with opportunities lost in the process. Either way, I had a century-old history and mission to lean upon when I was uncertain how to proceed, and I had a stellar team who knew the ins and outs of running the university.

In contrast, with the Knight-Hennessy Scholars, I am facing a challenge I haven't encountered since my days as an entrepreneur: a blank slate. Phil Knight and I began with an idea; now my team and I must make that dream real.

No one can tell us exactly how to build our program, or which scholars we should select, or which methods will cultivate leadership potential. We are writing our own mission statement. As yet we have no proof of concept, no prototype. Rather we will go into "production" with an untested model, on day one.

Hence, I am as thankful for my short tenure as a start-up founder at MIPS as I am for my years at Stanford. These days, I find myself living the life of an entrepreneur, wearing multiple hats each day—from advocate to ambassador to financial advisor to professor.

Thank goodness, once again, I have an incredibly talented staff devoted to our project, who handle the myriad phone calls we receive as we enter the final stages of the admissions process.

One of the lessons I learned as an entrepreneur is that success can be almost as dangerous as failure, especially when demand outpaces production. As of December 2017, the program has received more than 3,600 applications for the fifty scholarships in the inaugural class. They represent a truly global group of people, from over one hundred countries and distributed across 95 percent of the graduate programs at Stanford. Yet our acceptance rate will be less than 1.5 percent, below the rate for any other degree program at Stanford.

Unfortunately, a large number of applicants—many of them extraordinary by any measure—are going to be disappointed. Here the cascade of questions begins: Are we being *too* exclusive? Should we try to scale our cohort up to one hundred more quickly? How would that affect the quality of the program? Do we have the right criteria for making our selection, or are we failing to identify the X-factor that characterizes potentially great leaders? Is our curriculum right for the task at hand, or are we emphasizing the wrong things?

I wrote this book, in part, to explore the traits and practices I have learned—from highly respected leaders, and from my own, sometimes painful, experiences—that have proven critical to leading well. Some of these traits and practices are counterintuitive, while others simply diverge from orthodox views of leadership taught in schools and manuals. The question before us now is whether these traits can be taught, and if they can, how? I have no doubt that our scholars will be among the brightest people on the planet, but will the experiences we design for them help them build skills, enhance empathy, and prepare for future challenges and opportunities?

These questions remain to be answered. Of course, we will make mistakes. Thankfully, the last three decades have taught me not to fear mistakes, but instead to learn from them, make adjustments, and carry on. I have also learned, to paraphrase Dr. Martin Luther King Jr., you don't need to see the whole staircase to take the first step. So we will step forward, guided by wisdoms gained from the past and curiosity about the future.

I would not be here on the brink of this adventure without the friendship, the assistance, and the wise counsel of many people I have met along the way, some of whom I have mentioned in this book. One of those people has been by my side since we worked together in a King Kullen grocery store on Long Island almost fifty years ago: my wife, Andrea. Without her patience, empathy, incredible people skills, and support, I could not have accomplished most of what you have read here, nor reached this extraordinary moment. After more than forty years of her husband on the job, she might have expected to have him at home, tending to the garden or making valiant, if inept, attempts at plumbing repairs. Instead, I have taken on a new task that may keep me occupied for several years. It is a testament to her love and selflessness that she still supports me every step of the way, while helpfully reminding me that it is unlikely I will be at my best if I schedule myself as I did twenty years ago!

I deeply appreciate that Phil Knight believed in the program we are building and in me. Many others joined in to make the Knight-Hennessy Scholars possible, including Steve Denning, Bob King, Jerry Yang, Mike Volpe, Susan McCaw, John Gunn, Ram Shriram, and many others.

In January 2018, we brought 103 finalists to campus for a weekend, introducing them to Stanford and providing us with an opportunity to meet the candidates before we made our final selection. It was a wonderful weekend with excitement, exploration, and the joy of being with a community of people dedicated to making the world better. We then set out on the difficult task of narrowing the finalists down to our first cohort of 51 scholars. In mid-February 2018, I personally called each of the selected scholars. This stellar group of young people carry passports from twenty-one countries, hail from

21/51 = 41% foreign
(too high in my opinion!)

thirty-eight undergraduate institutions, and will enroll in degree pro-grams in all seven schools of the university.

The chance to help grow the next generation of world leaders—enlightened, empathetic, humble, and supremely competent—this is what inspires my team and me. I hope we will make the world a better place for our having been here. If most of us are remembered for only one thing in our lives, I hope this program is it for me.

CODA

Books from Which I Have Learned

"Books are the quietest and most constant of friends; they are the most
accessible and wisest of counselors, and the most patient of teachers."
Charles W. Eliot, longest-serving president of Harvard University

Following is a selection of books that I have read and learned from
over the years. The nonfiction books are organized by topic, and
within each topic, I have chosen one book as a significant example,
illustrating the insights I gained from it. In general, I prefer biographies and histories to leadership-focused books, though I do include
a small section of those that relate directly to the topics in this book.
At the end, I offer a short list of fiction writers who have informed
me, especially about issues of how we choose to live our lives.

Washington and His Times

David Hackett Fischer, *Washington's Crossing* (New York: Oxford
University Press, 2004)
A history of the pivotal time in the American Revolution when, af-
ter a series of defeats in New York, Washington went on the offensive.
(The crossing is both a personal crossing to a new strategy and the
literal crossing of the Delaware.) David McCullough's book discusses
the same time frame. All these books emphasize Washington's public
humility and his views on equality and meritocracy.
Ron Chernow, *Washington: A Life* (New York: Penguin Press, 2010)
David McCullough, *1776* (New York: Simon & Schuster, 2005)

Lincoln and His Times

Doris Kearns Goodwin, *Team of Rivals: The Political Genius of Abraham Lincoln* (New York: Simon & Schuster, 2006)

> Here I am forced to choose among a number of books that deeply affected me. I choose *Team of Rivals* for its brilliant discussion of team building, collaboration, humility, maintenance of a moral compass, and courage.

David Herbert Donald, *Lincoln* (New York: Simon & Schuster, 1996)

James McPherson, *Tried by War: Abraham Lincoln as Commander in Chief* (New York: Penguin Press, 2008)

William Lee Miller, *Lincoln's Virtues: An Ethical Biography* (New York: Vintage, 2003)

Ronald C. White Jr., *Lincoln's Greatest Speech: The Second Inaugural* (New York: Simon & Schuster, 2002)

Franklin Delano Roosevelt and His Times

David Kennedy, *Freedom from Fear: The American People in Depression and War, 1929–1945* (New York: Oxford University Press, 1999)

> This is a history book, rather than a biography, but FDR dominates the scene from his election in 1932 until his death. His fireside chats during the Depression, his actions to counteract the scourge of the Depression and unemployment, his relationship with Churchill and alliance with England, and his marshaling of the vast effort to win the war all demonstrate that FDR was a determined leader.

H. W. Brands, *Traitor to His Class: The Privileged Life and Radical Presidency of Franklin Delano Roosevelt* (New York: Anchor Books, 2008)

Doris Kearns Goodwin, *No Ordinary Time: Franklin and Eleanor Roosevelt—The Home Front in World War II* (New York: Simon & Schuster, 1994)

Jon Meacham, *Franklin and Winston: An Intimate Portrait of an Epic Friendship* (New York: Random House, 2003)

Other Presidents and Their Times

Edmund Morris, *The Rise of Theodore Roosevelt* (New York: Modern
  Library, 2001), *Theodore Rex* ((New York: Modern Library, 2002),
  Colonel Roosevelt (New York: Random House, 2010)

  Theodore Roosevelt was an amazing individual: athlete, intellectual,
  consummate reader, historian, adventurer, reformer, rancher, and im-
  probable president. He overcame poor health, reformed civil service,
  combatted the trusts, created the national park system, helped end the
  Russo-Japanese War, and explored the unknown Amazon headwaters
  when he was in his sixties. What a life.

H. W. Brands, *Andrew Jackson: His Life and Times* (New York:
  Doubleday, 2005)

Robert Caro, *Master of the Senate: The Years of Lyndon Johnson* (New
  York: Alfred A. Knopf, 2002)

Timothy Egan, *The Big Burn: Teddy Roosevelt and the Fire That Saved
  America* (New York: Mariner Books, 2010)

Joseph Ellis, *American Sphinx: The Character of Thomas Jefferson* (New
  York: Alfred A. Knopf, 1997)

Ulysses S. Grant, *The Personal Memoirs of U. S. Grant*, 3 volumes
  (Cambridge, Mass.: The Belknap Press of Harvard University
  Press, 2017)

David McCullough, *John Adams* (New York: Simon & Schuster,
  2001)

David McCullough, *Truman* (New York: Simon & Schuster, 1992)

Jack McLaughlin, *Jefferson and Monticello: The Biography of a Builder*
  (New York: Henry Holt, 1988)

U.S. Founders and Early Leaders and Their Times

H. W. Brands, *The First American: The Life and Times of Benjamin
  Franklin* (New York: Doubleday, 2000)

  Franklin was in some ways the most amazing of the founders: scientist, writer, and politician. He was a Renaissance man who came from
  humble beginnings. His Junto became the model for an intellectual society; his inventions from stoves to the glass harmonica were amazing.

He was a prolific and insightful writer. As a diplomat he probably did more to bring the French into the war than any other figure, and Yorktown was won on the strength of the French navy. There is much to be admired and much to be learned from "Old Ben."

Ron Chernow, *Alexander Hamilton* (New York: Penguin Press, 2004)

David Hackett Fischer, *Champlain's Dream* (New York: Simon & Schuster, 2008)

David Hackett Fischer, *Paul Revere's Ride* (New York: Oxford University Press, 1994)

Walter Isaacson, *Benjamin Franklin: An American Life* (New York: Simon & Schuster, 2003)

Jack Rakove, *Original Meanings: Politics and Ideas in the Making of the Constitution* (New York: Alfred A. Knopf, 1996)

Cokie Roberts, *Ladies of Liberty: The Women Who Shaped Our Nation* (New York: HarperCollins, 2016)

Other Leaders in the United States

David Garrow, *Bearing the Cross: Martin Luther King, Jr., and the Southern Christian Leadership Conference* (New York: HarperCollins, 1986)
This was a tough choice, as there are many worthwhile books in this section. I picked this biography of MLK because of its exploration of his path to leadership, which began reluctantly, and which encountered numerous setbacks. In the end, it is a story of a man rising to the call to leadership, despite the hazards he knew awaited him.

Sara Josephine Baker, *Fighting for Life* (New York: New York Review, 2013 [1939])

Kai Bird and Martin J. Sherwin, *American Prometheus: The Triumph and Tragedy of J. Robert Oppenheimer* (New York: Alfred J. Knopf, 2005)

Elisabeth Bumiller, *Condoleezza Rice: An American Life: A Biography* (New York: Random House, 2007, 2009)

Robert Caro, *The Power Broker: Robert Moses and the Fall of New York* (New York: Alfred A. Knopf, 1974)

Ron Chernow, *Titan: The Story of John D. Rockefeller, Jr.* (New York: Random House, 1998)

Katharine Graham, *Personal History* (New York: Alfred A. Knopf, 1997)

Laura Hillenbrand, *Unbroken: A World War II Story of Survival, Resilience, and Redemption* (New York: Random House, 2010)

Walter Isaacson, *Kissinger: A Biography* (New York: Simon & Schuster, 1992, 2005)

Phil Knight, *Shoe Dog: A Memoir by the Creator of Nike* (New York: Scribner, 2016)

William Manchester, *American Caesar: Douglas MacArthur 1880–1964* (New York: Little, Brown, 1978)

Lynne Olson, *Citizens of London: The Americans Who Stood with Britain in Its Darkest, Finest Hour* (New York: Random House, 2010)

Condoleezza Rice, *Extraordinary, Ordinary People: A Memoir of Family* (New York: Three Rivers Press, 2011)

William Tecumseh Sherman, *Memoirs of General W. T. Sherman* (New York: Penguin, 2000 [1875])

T. J. Stiles, *The First Tycoon: The Epic Life of Cornelius Vanderbilt* (New York: Alfred A. Knopf, 2009)

Booker T. Washington, *Up from Slavery: An Autobiography* (various editions; first published New York: Doubleday, 1901)

U.S. History: Nineteenth Century

Daniel Walker Howe, *What Hath God Wrought: The Transformation of America, 1815–1848* (Oxford, UK; New York: Oxford University Press, 2007)

I am a devoted reader of the *Oxford History of the United States*, and most of the books in the series appear somewhere in this Coda. Howe's book covers the period from the rise of Andrew Jackson to the Mexican-American War. It is the story of the rapid growth and diversification of the United States; the influence of religion in society's development; and deep divides over slavery, women's rights, and the war with Mexico.

Stephen Ambrose, *Nothing Like It in the World: The Men Who Built the Transcontinental Railroad, 1863–1869* (New York: Simon & Schuster, 2000)

Alexis de Tocqueville, *Democracy in America, Volumes I and II* (various editions; originally published 1835 and 1840)

James M. McPherson, *Battle Cry of Freedom: The Civil War Era* (Oxford, UK; New York: Oxford University Press, 1988)

Louis Menand, *The Metaphysical Club: A Story of Ideas in America* (New York: Farrar, Straus and Giroux, 2001)

Mark Twain, *Life on the Mississippi* (various editions; first published 1883)

Richard White, *Railroaded: The Transcontinentals and the Making of Modern America* (New York: W.W. Norton, 2011)

Gordon S. Wood, *Empire of Liberty: A History of the Early Republic, 1789–1815* (Oxford, UK; New York: Oxford University Press, 2009)

Richard Zacks, *The Pirate Coast: Thomas Jefferson, The First Marines, and the Secret Mission of 1805* (New York: Hyperion, 2005)

U.S. History: Twentieth Century

David Halberstam, *The Coldest Winter: America and the Korean War* (New York: Hyperion, 2007)

Halberstam is well known for his history of the Vietnam War (*The Best and the Brightest*), but this book shows that America's deceptions about winning wars began with the Korean War in the aftermath of World War II. There were massive mistakes, including little preparation for the Korean winter; MacArthur's miscalculation of Chinese intervention, which led to great losses and an eventual stalemate; and MacArthur's public arguments with President Truman, which led to his being fired. It was arguably the first of a number of U.S. failures in foreign wars, all launched for preemptive or political reasons.

Rick Atkinson, *An Army at Dawn: The War in North Africa, 1942–1943* (New York: Henry Holt, 2002); *The Day of Battle: The War in Sicily and Italy, 1943–1944* (New York: Henry Holt, 2007); *The Guns*

at Last Light: The War in Western Europe, 1944–1945 (New York:
   Picador, 2013)
Jonathan R. Cole, *The Great American University: Its Rise to Preeminence,*
   Its Indispensable National Role, Why It Must Be Protected (New York:
   PublicAffairs, 2009, 2012)
David M. Kennedy, *The American People in World War II: Freedom from*
   Fear, Part II (Oxford, UK; New York: Oxford University Press,
   1999)
Richard Rhodes, *The Making of the Atomic Bomb* (New York:
   Touchstone, 1988)
Ted Sorensen, *Counselor: A Life on the Edge of History* (Norwalk, CT:
   Easton Press, 2008)

Other Leaders Around the World: Ancient Times

Donald Kagan, *Pericles of Athens and the Birth of Democracy* (New York:
   Free Press, 1991)
   I read this book after I read Kagan's one-volume history of the Pelo-
   ponnesian War. Pericles was a dominant leader for thirty years during
   the Golden Age of Athens, when democracy expanded, Athens was
   growing in influence and economic power, the arts thrived, and proj-
   ects such as the Parthenon were undertaken.
Anthony Everitt, *Augustus: The Life of Rome's First Emperor* (New York:
   Random House, 2006)
Harold Lamb, *Alexander of Macedon* (various editions; first published
   New York: Doubleday, 1946)
Harold Lamb, *Hannibal: One Man Against Rome* (various editions; first
   published 1958)
Richard Winston, *Charlemagne* (various editions; first published
   London: Eyre & Spottiswoode, 1956)

Other Leaders Around the World: Modern Times

Robert K. Massie, *Peter the Great: His Life and World* (New York: Alfred A. Knopf, 1980)

Peter the Great took Russia from backwards medieval country to leading European state. He began this journey by getting out and learning about the rest of Europe, including traveling for study and apprenticing as a shipwright. His determination to bring Russia into the modern age, despite much opposition, was amazing, as was his willingness to ask for help, to humble himself, despite being the tsar of all Russia.

Mohandas K. Gandhi, *An Autobiography: The Story of My Experiments with Truth* (Boston: Beacon Press, 1993 [1957])

Roy Jenkins, *Churchill: A Biography* (New York: Macmillan, 2001))

Nelson Mandela, *Long Walk to Freedom: The Autobiography of Nelson Mandela* (New York: Little, Brown, 1994, 1995)

Robert K. Massie, *Catherine the Great: Portrait of a Woman* (New York: Random House, 2011)

Andrew Roberts, *Napoleon: A Life* (New York: Penguin, 2014, 2015)

Leaders and Adventure

Alfred Lansing, *Endurance: Shackleton's Incredible Voyage* (various editions; first published 1959)

Ernest Shackleton's journey is surely one of the greatest leadership adventure stories ever. Trapped in the polar ice of Antarctica, his ship is destroyed. He leads his men across two ocean journeys totaling over a thousand miles on open seas—in lifeboats. Shackleton's leadership and team-building skills were critical to this daring journey and helped him complete the rescue without losing a man.

Daniel James Brown, *The Boys in the Boat: Nine Americans and Their Epic Quest for Gold at the 1936 Berlin Olympics* (New York: Penguin, 2014)

Maurice Herzog, *Annapurna: The First Conquest of an 8,000-Meter Peak* (New York: Lyons Press, 1997 [1952])

T. E. Lawrence, *Seven Pillars of Wisdom* (various editions; first published 1935)

Nathaniel Philbrick, *In the Heart of the Sea: The Tragedy of the Whaleship* Essex (New York: Viking Penguin, 2000)

Innovators: Renaissance Through the Eighteenth Century

Walter Isaacson, *Leonardo da Vinci* (New York: Simon & Schuster, 2017)

In a book about the man who could claim to be the inspiration for the term "Renaissance man," Isaacson lays out Leonardo's life as an inventor, artist, and scientist who is driven by curiosity. Despite the numerous unfinished projects (a habit of Leonardo's), he left an indelible mark on our world.

Ross King, *Brunelleschi's Dome: How a Renaissance Genius Reinvented Architecture* (New York: Bloomsbury, 2000)

James Reston, Jr., *Galileo: A Life* (New York: HarperCollins, 1994)

Dava Sobel, *Longitude: The True Story of a Lone Genius Who Solved the Greatest Scientific Problem of His Time* (New York: Walker, 1995)

Innovators: Nineteenth Century

Janet Browne, *Charles Darwin: Voyaging* (Princeton, NJ: Princeton University Press, 1996)

Darwin is a fascinating figure. He had a hard time finding his calling in science and was desperately seasick during much of the voyage of the *Beagle*, but his scientific curiosity and meticulous observation and recording enabled him to discover and document one of the fundamental tenets underlying life.

David McCullough, *The Great Bridge: The Epic Story of the Building of the Brooklyn Bridge* (New York: Simon & Schuster, 2012)

David McCullough, *The Path Between the Seas: The Creation of the Panama Canal, 1870–1914* (New York: Simon & Schuster, 1977)

Witold Rybczynski, *A Clearing in the Distance: Frederick Law Olmsted and America in the 19th Century* (New York: Touchstone, 2000)

Marc J. Seifer, *Wizard: The Life and Times of Nicola Tesla: Biography of a Genius* (New York: Citadel, 1998)

Randall Stross, *The Wizard of Menlo Park: How Thomas Alva Edison Invented the Modern World* (New York: Three Rivers Press, 2007)

Innovators: Twentieth Century

David McCullough, *The Wright Brothers* (New York: Simon &
    Schuster, 2015)
    I love McCullough's books about innovators and innovations, and this
    one is a gem. The Wright brothers combined passion, curiosity, perse-
    verance, and vision. Their focus on understanding the mechanisms of
    flight and on the problem of control was central to their success.

Leslie Berlin, *Troublemakers: Silicon Valley's Coming of Age* (New York:
    Simon & Schuster, 2017)

Andrew Hodges, *Alan Turing: The Enigma of Intelligence* (New York:
    HarperCollins, 1985)

Walter Isaacson, *The Innovators: How a Group of Hackers, Geniuses, and
    Geeks Created the Digital Revolution* (New York: Simon & Schuster,
    2014)

Walter Isaacson, *Steve Jobs* (New York: Simon & Schuster, 2011)

Michael S. Malone, *Bill & Dave: How Hewlett and Packard Built the
    World's Greatest Company* (New York: Portfolio, 2007)

Michael S. Malone, *The Intel Trinity: How Robert Noyce, Gordon Moore,
    and Andy Grove Built the World's Most Important Company* (New York:
    HarperCollins, 2014)

*Science, Math, and Technology: History and Development
(including the social sciences)*

Siddhartha Mukherjee, *The Emperor of All Maladies: A Biography of
    Cancer* (New York: Scribner, 2010)
    Mukherjee's story of the history of cancer treatment is riveting and
    provides deep insights into the nature of the disease, as well as the dif-
    ficulty of medical advances.

Bill Bryson, *A Short History of Nearly Everything* (New York: Broadway,
    2003)

Stephen Hawking, *A Brief History of Time* (New York: Bantam, 1988)

Douglas Hofstadter, *Gödel, Escher, Bach: An Eternal Golden Braid* (New
    York: Vintage, 1979)

Daniel Kahneman, *Thinking, Fast and Slow* (New York: Farrar, Straus and Giroux, 2011)

Manjit Kumar, *Quantum: Einstein, Bohr, and the Great Debate About the Nature of Reality* (New York: W.W. Norton, 2008)

Leonard Mlodinow, *Euclid's Window: The Story of Geometry from Parallel Lines to Hyperspace* (New York: Touchstone, 2001)

Siddhartha Mukherjee, *The Gene: An Intimate History* (New York: Scribner, 2016)

Robert Sapolsky, *Monkeyluv: And Other Lessons on Our Lives as Animals* (New York: Vintage, 2006)

Robert Sapolsky, *Why Zebras Don't Get Ulcers: A Guide to Stress, Stress-Related Diseases, and Coping* (various editions; first published New York: W.H. Freeman, 1994)

Nate Silver, *The Signal and the Noise: Why So Many Predictions Fail—but Some Don't* (New York: Penguin, 2012, 2015)

Leonard Susskind, *The Black Hole War: My Battle with Stephen Hawking to Make the World Safe for Quantum Mechanics* (New York: Little, Brown, 2008)

Lewis Thomas, *A Long Line of Cells: Collected Essays* (n.p.: Book of the Month Club, 1990)

Neil deGrasse Tyson, *Astrophysics for People in a Hurry* (New York: W.W. Norton, 2017)

A Life Worth Living (also see the fiction list)

David Brooks, *The Road to Character* (New York: Random House, 2015)
This was also a tough choice; there are lots of good and very moving books in this section. I choose this book because it tells stories of the development of leaders from Frances Perkins to Dwight Eisenhower to Dorothy Day. Many of the aspects of leadership that I believe are important are embedded in the lives of the people Brooks profiles.

Saint Aurelius Augustinus, *Confessions of Saint Augustine* (various editions; see, for example, London; New York: Penguin, 1961)

Marcus Aurelius, *Meditations* (various editions; often based on George Long translation, first published London: Bell, 1962)

Anthony Doerr, *Four Seasons in Rome: On Twins, Insomnia, and the Biggest Funeral in the History of the World* (New York: Scribner, 2007)

Anne Frank, *The Diary of a Young Girl* (various editions; first copyrighted 1952)

Atul Gawande, *Being Mortal: Medicine and What Matters in the End* (New York: Metropolitan, 2014)

Paul Kalanithi, *When Breath Becomes Air* (New York: Random House, 2016)

Randy Pausch, with Jeffrey Zaslow, *The Last Lecture* (New York: Hyperion, 2008)

Abraham Verghese, *My Own Country: A Doctor's Story* (New York: Simon & Shuster, 1994)

Abraham Verghese, *The Tennis Partner* (New York: HarperCollins, 1998)

Elie Wiesel, *Night* (various editions; see, for example, New York: Hill and Wang, 1972, 1985, 2006)

World History: Ancient

John R. Hale, *Lords of the Sea: The Epic Story of the Athenian Navy and the Birth of Democracy* (New York: Viking, 2009)

John Hale is both a great writer and a great speaker. His book on the history of Athens taught me many things. Athens was arguably the first great civilization to be heavily reliant on trade (Rome would follow), but it was also a democracy, one in which ordinary citizens manned the galleys and defended their homeland.

Edward Gibbon, *The History of the Decline and Fall of the Roman Empire* (various editions; first published 1776–1789)

Herodotus, *The Persian Wars* (various editions)

Donald Kagan, *The Peloponnesian War* (New York: Viking, 2003)

Barbara Mertz, *Temples, Tombs & Hieroglyphs: A Popular History of Ancient Egypt* (New York: Dodd, Mead, 1964)

Ian Shaw (editor), *The Oxford History of Ancient Egypt* (Oxford, UK; New York: Oxford University Press, 2000)

Thucydides, *The History of the Peloponnesian War* (various editions)

World History: Early Modern to Modern

Barbara W. Tuchman, *A Distant Mirror: The Calamitous 14th Century* (New York: Ballantine, 1978)

> Tuchman's history of the fourteenth century, with its tragic wars, harsh lives, and imperious feudal society, shows the veneer of chivalry for what it likely was, a class distinction without much merit.

Roger Crowley, *City of Fortune: How Venice Ruled the Seas* (New York: Random House, 2012)

Roger Crowley, *Empires of the Sea: The Siege of Malta, the Battle of Lepanto, and the Contest for the Center of the World* (New York: Random House, 2008)

Roger Crowley, *1453: The Holy War for Constantinople and the Clash of Islam and the West* (New York: Hyperion, 2006)

Dominic Greene, *Three Empires on the Nile: The Victorian Jihad, 1869–1899* (New York: Free Press, 2007)

Timothy E. Gregory, *A History of Byzantium* (Malden, MA: Blackwell, 2005)

World History: Twentieth Century

Margaret MacMillan, *Paris 1919: Six Months That Changed the World* (New York: Random House, 2002)

> Greed rather than humility was the story of the Paris peace conference. The European allied powers' vengeance, combined with Wilson's ineffectiveness, led to impossible reparations imposed on Germany, which created the environment that allowed Hitler to rise to power. Together with Tuchman's volume on the origins of the first world war, these two books illustrate the foibles that started the war and led to a deeply unfortunate ending.

Liaquat Ahamed, *Lords of Finance: The Bankers Who Broke the World*
(New York: Penguin, 2009)

Robert K. Massie, *Nicholas and Alexandra: The Classic Account of the
Fall of the Romanov Dynasty* (New York: Atheneum, 1967)

Barbara W. Tuchman, *The Guns of August* (New York: Macmillan,
1962)

History of Civilization and Its Development:
Ancient and Modern

Jared Diamond, *Guns, Germs, and Steel: The Fates of Human Societies*
(New York: W.W. Norton, 1999)

Diamond's book poses an interesting hypothesis, namely that geo-
graphic and other natural factors, rather than cultural differences, have
led to vastly different outcomes for societies. Some of Diamond's examples are quite compelling, and in other cases, the argument does not
seem to work. For an interesting comparison, read Ferguson's book on
the development of civilization and its equally compelling examples of
the difference that cultural and legal systems made. Both approaches
seem to offer good, if incomplete, themes.

Karen Armstrong, *A History of God: The 4,000-Year Quest of Judaism,
Christianity and Islam* (New York: Ballantine, 1993)

Niall Ferguson, *The Ascent of Money: A Financial History of the World*
(New York: Penguin, 2008)

Niall Ferguson, *Civilization: The West and the Rest* (New York: Penguin,
2012)

Thomas L. Friedman, *The World Is Flat: A Brief History of the Twenty-
First Century* (New York: Farrar, Straus and Giroux, 2005, 2006)

Hilda Hookham, *A Short History of China* (New York: New American
Library, 1972)

Steven Pinker, *The Better Angels of Our Nature: Why Violence Has
Declined* (New York: Viking, 2011)

Barbara W. Tuchman, *The March of Folly: From Troy to Vietnam* (New
York: Alfred A. Knopf, 1984)

Fareed Zakaria, *The Post-American World* (New York: W.W. Norton, 2008)

Leadership in Corporations, Government, and Academia

John W. Gardner, *Living, Leading, and the American Dream* (San Francisco: Jossey-Bass, 2003)

Gardner found success in leadership positions in government, the non-profit world, and the academy. His quote, "We are all faced with a series of great opportunities—brilliantly disguised as insoluble problems," has always inspired me. As secretary of HEW, a Republican serving LBJ, he was the lead architect in the creation of Medicare. He stood by his principles and resigned his cabinet position because he could not support the Vietnam War. He founded Common Cause and led the creation of the Corporation for Public Broadcasting. I met him shortly before his death at a small lunch, which I'll never forget. Gardner's book is a set of lessons on leadership taken from his wide-ranging experiences.

Warren Bennis, *On Becoming a Leader* (Rev. ed., New York: Basic Books, 2003)

William G. Bowen, ed. Kevin M. Guthrie, *Ever the Leader: Selected Writings 1995–2016* (Princeton, NJ: Princeton University Press, 2018)

Kevin Cashman, *Leadership from the Inside Out: Becoming a Leader for Life* (3rd ed., Oakland: Berrett-Koehler, 2017)

Gerhard Casper, *The Winds of Freedom: Addressing Challenges to the University* (New Haven, CT: Yale University Press, 2014)

Stephen Covey, *The 7 Habits of Highly Effective People: Powerful Lessons in Personal Change* (New York: Simon & Schuster, 1989, 2004)

Robert M. Gates, *A Passion for Leadership: Lessons on Change and Reform from Fifty Years of Public Service* (New York: Vintage, 2016)

Bill George and Peter Sims, *True North: Discover Your Authentic Leadership* (2nd ed., San Francisco: Jossey-Bass, 2015)

Robert K. Greenleaf, *Servant Leadership: A Journey into the Nature of Legitimate Power & Greatness* (New York: Paulist Press, 2002)

Vartan Gregorian, *The Road to Home: My Life and Times* (New York: Simon & Schuster, 2003)

Fiction Authors from Whom I Have Learned

Dante Alighieri, for the *Divine Comedy*, especially *Inferno*.

Isaac Asimov, for the Foundation and Robot novels, stories of what it means to be human, told in the far future.

Jane Austen, for her writing, her characters, and the insightful depiction of human emotion, particularly its role in decisions.

The Brontë sisters, for their family legacy: *Jane Eyre*, *Wuthering Heights*, and *The Tenant of Wildfell Hall*.

Willa Cather, for novels of the American West.

Wilkie Collins, for great mysteries probing human emotion and motivations.

A. J. Cronin, for moving novels of human sacrifice and endurance.

Charles Dickens, for his use of language, his characters, and his stories of the evils of English society. *A Tale of Two Cities* remains one of my favorite novels of all time. Dickens's treatment of issues of justice, love, endurance, and self-sacrifice is timeless. The opening sentence is one of the greatest in any novel.

Theodore Dreiser, for his novels of personal choice leading to tragedy.

George Eliot (Mary Ann Evans), for incredible novels depicting complex characters and the role of human emotion.

Elizabeth Gaskell, for her stories of the horrors of the poor during the Industrial Revolution and the triumph of love.

Thomas Hardy, for novels that depict the full range of human behavior from good to evil and the triumph of good over evil.

Frank Herbert, for his creative depiction of technology and fantastic worlds and the struggle of good, evil, leadership, and sacrifice in the Dune series.

Homer, for *The Iliad* and *The Odyssey*, two of the great stories that blend adventure with moral and ethical decisions.

Victor Hugo, for two great stories of evil and the triumph of
    righteousness.

Henry James, for novels about romance, pride, and human
    psychology.

Ayn Rand, for her depictions of ambition, the value of free
    enterprise and personal gain, and (for me) the negative
    consequences.

Shakespeare, for his illumination of human emotions spanning
    comedy, history, and tragedy.

Wallace Stegner, for his novels of the American West and for
    founding the Stanford Creative Writing Program.

John Steinbeck, for his stories about human character and
    challenges, told with empathy and humor.

J. R. R. Tolkien, for his creative fantasy and deep story of good and
    evil in the Lord of the Rings trilogy.

Anthony Trollope, for his novels of social and gender issues in
    Victorian England, especially the Chronicles of Barsetshire.

Mark Twain, for humor and pathos; arguably the greatest
    American novelist.

ACKNOWLEDGMENTS

My spouse and partner, Andrea, has been my life instructor for almost fifty years. She taught me to appreciate the visual arts, to remember to acknowledge and thank people, and to be humble (after all, she knew me when I was a stock-boy in a grocery store).

I have had the opportunity to work with extraordinary people in my life, starting with my graduate students and faculty colleagues. Their dedication to excellence and their creativity made me a better researcher and teacher. I worked with terrific leaders at Silicon Graphics, MIPS, and Atheros, where I learned lessons at the frantic pace that characterizes start-ups in Silicon Valley. I also worked with extraordinary academic leaders: Jim Gibbons as dean of Engineering, Condi Rice as provost, and Gerhard Casper as president. Serving with extraordinary people on the boards of Cisco and Google helped me understand how to operate effectively in large organizations.

As president of Stanford, I collaborated with an outstanding team of deans and vice presidents. My academic partner, Provost John Etchemendy, was, I believe, the best provost in higher education in the United States.

I also worked with over seventy different trustees during my sixteen years as president. I had four dedicated and inspiring chairs of the board: Steve Denning, Leslie Hume, Burt McMurtry, and Isaac Stein. In addition, Peter Bing, Stanford's longest-serving trustee, was a source of invaluable wisdom over the years.

I could not possibly have gotten this book done without the help of the team at Silicon Valley Press: Joe DiNucci, Cheryl Dumesnil, Atiya Dwyer, and Mike Malone. Jim Levine and his team at Levine, Greenberg, Rostan represented the author and the book well. The team at Stanford University Press was a pleasure to work with. A special thank you to Walter Isaacson for his insightful foreword. I also benefited from the advice of several people who read early drafts: Peter Bing, Steve Denning, John Etchemendy, Andrea Hennessy, Burt McMurtry, Charles Prober, Condoleezza Rice, Isaac Stein, and Phil Taubman. Jeff Wachtel, who served as my very able, special assistant when I was provost and president, and has joined me on the Knight-Hennessy team, provided invaluable feedback; after all, he was there at many of the most challenging moments in those seventeen years.

NOTES

Introduction

1. See Robert K. Greenleaf, *Servant Leadership: A Journey into the Nature of Legitimate Power & Greatness*, 25th anniv. ed. (New York: Paulist Press, 2002), Chapter 1, 28–60.

2. See John W. Gardner, *Living, Leading, and the American Dream* (San Francisco: Jossey-Bass, 2003), Part Two: "The Courage to Live and Learn," 41–112.

Chapter 1: Humility

1. See Warren Bennis, *On Becoming a Leader*, Rev. ed. (New York: Basic Books, 2003), Chapter 3, 91–108.

2. See David Herbert Donald, *Lincoln*, 1st ed. (New York: Simon & Shuster, 1996), Chapters 9 and 19; Doris Kearns Goodwin, *Team of Rivals: The Political Genius of Abraham Lincoln* (New York: Simon & Schuster, 2006), Chapter 3.

Chapter 2: Authenticity and Trust

1. See Bennis, *On Becoming a Leader*, Chapter 2, 74–90; Bill George and Peter Sims, *True North: Discover Your Authentic Leadership*, 2nd ed. (San Francisco: Jossey-Bass, 2015), Chapter 4, 91–114.

2. See Kevin Cashman, *Leadership from the Inside Out: Becoming a Leader for Life*, 3rd ed., rev. (Oakland: Berrett-Koehler, 2017), 193–194.

3. See Cashman, *Leadership from the Inside Out*, 41–45.

4. See Cashman, *Leadership from the Inside Out*, 51–53.

5. See William Lee Miller, *Lincoln's Virtues: An Ethical Biography* (New York: Vintage, 2003), Chapters 8, 11, 14.

6. See Condoleeza Rice, *Extraordinary, Ordinary People: A Memoir of Family* (New York: Three Rivers Press, 2011), 14–15.

Chapter 3: Leadership as Service

1. See Greenleaf, *Servant Leadership*, Chapter 1, 29–61.

2. See Greenleaf, *Servant Leadership*, Chapters 2, 4, 5, 6.

Chapter 4: Empathy

1. See Gardner, *Living, Leading, and the American Dream*, Chapter 16, 159–173.

2. See Sara Josephine Baker, *Fighting for Life* (New York: New York Review, 2013 [1939]), Chapter 1, 24.

Chapter 5: Courage

1. See Gardner, *Living, Leading, and the American Dream*, Chapter 16, 159–173; George and Sim, *True North*, 122–130; Cashman, *Leadership from the Inside Out*, 103–117.

2. See Bennis, *On Becoming a Leader*, Chapters 5 and 9.

Chapter 6: Collaboration and Teamwork

1. See Cashman, *Leadership from the Inside Out*, 23–25 (and elsewhere, scattered).

2. See Bennis, *On Becoming a Leader*, "Introduction to the Revised Edition," 2003.

3. See Greenleaf, *Servant Leadership*, Chapter 3, 81–115.

4. See Bennis, *On Becoming a Leader*, 130–135.

Chapter 8: Intellectual Curiosity

1. See Bennis, *On Becoming a Leader*, Chapter 4.

2. See David Hackett Fischer, *Washington's Crossing*, reprint ed. (New York: Oxford University Press, 2006), 7–50.

Chapter 9: Storytelling

1. See Cashman, *Leadership from the Inside Out*, Chapter 2, 70–77.

INDEX

abolitionism, 32
Adams, John, ix
Adams, Samuel, ix
admissions, 57
advisory roles, 40–41
Airbnb, 103
alcohol, 28
Alphabet/Google. *See* Google
AlphaGo, 118
Alta Vista, 105
alumni, 30, 58, 81, 145
Amy Blue Awards, 48–49
Anderson, Hunk, 91
Anderson, Moo, 91
Anderson, Putter, 91
Anderson Collection at Stanford
  University, 92, 147
Andreessen, Marc, 12–13
Apple Computer, 2, 110, 111, 135
Arrillaga, John, 90–91
artificial corneas, 131–32
artificial intelligence (AI), 60, 118
arts initiatives, 91, 112–14, 145, 147–48
Asimov, Isaac, 101
athletics, 7, 90, 129, 132
authenticity, 6, 21–34
awards, 48–49, 112, 128, 142

Baker, Sara Josephine, 62–63
basic research, 106
Baum, Frank, 119
Bay of Pigs invasion, 123
Bell, Gordon, 33

Bezos, Jeff, xi, 86
Bing, Peter, 137–38
Bing Concert Hall, 137–38, 147
bioengineering, 13, 133
biotechnology, 107
Bio-X, 13, 15, 131, 133
blame, 123
Booker, Cory, 128
Bradley, Bill, 128
brainstorming, 86
bravery, 65, 66
Brin, Sergey, 105, 109, 132, 135
Built to Last (Collins and Porras), 134
Bush, George W., 15
buzzwords, 22–23

Cantor Art Museum, 147
Cardinal Free Clinics, 43, 45
Cardinal Quarter, 47
career paths, 31–32
Caro, Robert, 121
Carroll, Lewis, 127
Casper, Gerhard, 4–5, 13, 34
cellular phones, 2–3, 104
change, 7; accelerating pace of, 76–77; in
  business vs. academia, 101–2. *See also*
  innovation
Chernow, Ron, 14
Cisco Systems, 5, 147
Civil War, 144
Clark, Jim, 3, 12–16, 88–89, 131
Clark Center, 15–16
climate change, 29

collaboration, xi, 7; celebrating successes of,
    98–99; failures of, 96–97; ground rules
    for, 87; hierarchy vs., 83–85, 87; leader's
    role in, 88–90, 94–96; multidisciplinary,
    13, 85, 87, 111, 112, 114, 131–32, 133;
    recruiting for, 85–86; unconventional
    kinds of, 90–92; upward, 92–94
college advising, 57
college sports, 7, 90, 129, 132
Collins, Jim, 134
Community Law Clinic, 43, 45
computer-aided design, 86
Computer System Laboratory, 3
confidence, 9
constituencies, 36–37; internal vs. external, 27
construction projects, 90–91
corneal transplants, 131–32
corporate boards, 5, 28
courage, 6, 65–82; bravery distinguished
    from, 65–66
Crane, Vaemond, 19–20
CUNY (City University of New York), 79

da Vinci, Leonardo, xi, 120
de Kooning, Willem, 91
delegating responsibility, 94
Denning, Roberta, 130, 146
Denning, Steve, 93, 127, 130, 146, 150,
    156
Denning House, 130, 146, 153
development economics, 47
Diamond, Larry, 47
Diebenkorn, Richard, 91
Digital Equipment Corporation (DEC),
    32–33
Diller, Scofidio, and Renfro (architectural
    firm), 148
disadvantaged students, 55, 57, 68
disaster relief, 53
divestment, 29
donors. *See* fundraising
Dream Act, 72
drinking, 28

East Palo Alto, Calif., 44
eBay, 103
Einstein, Albert, x, 84, 117, 124
Eisenhower, Dwight, 123

Emancipation Proclamation, 32
empathy, xi, 6, 25; equity vs., 56–58; in future
    leaders, 61–63; importance of, 51–53; as
    learning opportunity, 55–56; perceptive,
    60–61; personal vs. institutional, 53–55;
    with team members, 59–60
endowments, 29, 67, 101, 139
enrollment, 96–97, 124
environmental sustainability, 112, 139, 148
Etchemendy, John, 5, 88–90, 91

Feeney, Chuck, 16
Festschrifts, 142
fiduciary duty, 93
Filo, Dave, 132
financial aid, 51–52, 54, 57–58, 68, 139,
    145, 148
firing, 24, 26, 60
Ford, Henry, 83
fossil fuels, 29
Francis, Sam, 91
Frank, Anne, 153
Franklin, Benjamin, ix, x, xi, 123
Frohmayer, David, 128
fundraising, 11–12, 53, 93–94, 111; trust
    and, 30; storytelling and, 136–37

Gandhi, Mahatma, 9
Gates, Bill, xi, 56
Gates, Melinda, 56
Gawande, Atul, 128
General Use Permit, 70
Gettysburg Address, 73, 145
Ghana, 47
Gibbons, Jim, 36
goals, 39
Gomes, Peter, 136
Google, 5; ads vs. search results and,
    29–30, 105; artificial intelligence focus
    of, 118; creativity cultivated by, 109;
    innovations of, 104, 105, 111; Stanford
    linked to, 132, 133
"Google memo," 72
government service, 40
Grant, Ulysses S., 123, 144
Great Recession, 18, 66, 67, 78, 97
Grove, Andrew, 135
growth, 96–97, 124

Gunn, John, 156
Guston, Philip, 91

Haas, Peter, 46
Haas Center for Public Service, 46
Harvard Business School, 22
Hamilton, Alexander, 14
Hass, Mimi, 46
health care, 56, 62–63, 112, 139, 148
Hennessy, Andrea, 156
Hewlett, William, 132, 133, 146–47
Hewlett-Packard, 133, 135
hiring freezes, 67
Hockfield, Susan, 72
Homestead Act (1862), 144
housing, 91
Hoxby, Caroline, 57
humanities, 121, 143
Huang, Jensen, 133
Hume, Leslie, 81, 93
humility, x–xi, 6, 37; ambition and, 18;
    developing, 16–18; examples of, 12–16;
    failed collaborations and, 96; through
    fundraising, 11–12; personal growth
    through, 19–20; sources of, 9–10

IBM, 32, 111
immunization, 56
incrementalism, 67, 103, 104
incubators, 106, 107
India, 47
Industrial Revolution, 60
information technology, 107
innovation, 7, 128; in business vs.
    academia, 102, 106–8; decay of, 109;
    freedom of, 102–3; managing, 108–10;
    partners in, 105–6; start-ups driven by,
    103–5; strategic planning and, 110–15,
    131. See also change
integrity, 21
Intel, 2, 102, 135
intellectual curiosity, 7, 117–25
international relations, 112, 139
Internet, 2–3, 13
iPhone, 104, 110
Irish Potato Famine, 10
Isaacson, Walter, 120, 123–24, 128
James, William, 139

Jefferson, Thomas, ix
Jobs, Steve, x, xi, 24, 104, 110, 123,
    134–35
Johnson, Lyndon, 121, 123
Jordan, David Starr, 39
Joss, Bob, 113

K–12 initiative, 114
Kennedy, Don, 46
Kennedy, John F., 123
Kenya, 47
King, Bob, 47, 156
King, Dottie, 47
King, Martin Luther, Jr., 156
Knight, Phil, 5–6, 7, 128–29, 150–51, 154,
    156
Knight-Hennessy Scholars, 6, 28, 82,
    128–30, 141, 149–51, 153, 155–57;
    leadership focus of, 8, 61, 125; selectivity
    of, 138, 155; as start-up, 149–50

layoffs, 17, 24, 66, 67, 68
League of Nations, 145
learning, 7, 55–56, 117–25; from mistakes,
    95, 123, 124, 155–56
Lee, Harper, 51
legacy-building, 139–51
licensing, 107
Lincoln, Abraham, 21, 22, 65, 121;
    achievements of, 144; ambition and
    humility of, 18; as commander-in-chief,
    122, 140; as orator, 71, 73; slavery
    viewed by, 32
LinkedIn, 135–36
living wage, 74
loan forgiveness, 54, 55
long-term focus, 37–39
Lowell, A. Lawrence, 136
low-income students, 55, 57, 68
Lucille Packard Children's Hospital, 61
luck, 9–10

machine learning, 60
Macintosh computer, 110, 111
Madison, James, ix
Mandela, Nelson, 35
Master of the Senate (Caro), 121
McCaw, Susan, 156

McClellan, George B., 122, 140
McFaul, Michael, 128
McMurtry, Burt, 93, 147–48
McMurtry, Deedee, 147–48
McMurtry Art Building, 148
medical diagnostics, 60
Meehan, Bill, 149
meetings, 86
microprocessors, 3, 32, 86, 102–3
Miller, Bob, 17
miniaturization, 102
MIPS Computer Systems, 12, 85, 124,
    154; founding of, 16–17, 31, 33;
    innovation at, 102–3; layoffs at, 66;
    leadership roles at, 19–20, 88; setbacks
    at, 3, 110; teamwork at, 87–88
mission creep, 56–57
mission statements, 52
mistakes, 88; admitting, 20, 66, 97, 123;
    learning from, 95, 123, 124, 155–56; by
    subordinates, 59
Moore, Gordon, 135
Moore's Law, 102
Morgridge, John, 147
Morgridge, Tashia, 147
Morrill, Charles, 144
Morrill (Land Grant) College Act (1862),
    144
Mosaic browser, 13
Motherwell, Robert, 91
Motorola, 102
Mukherjee, Siddhartha, 128
Musk, Elon, 135

nanoscience, 133
NCAA, 129, 132
need-blind admissions, 57
Netscape, 13, 14
neuroscience, 118
New York campus proposal, 27, 77–82, 97,
    110, 124
New York Review of Books, 121
NeXT computer, 110
Nike, 5, 128
9/11 attacks, 18, 66, 70–71
Nobel Prize, 48, 112, 128
No Child Left Behind, 54

nonprofits, 7, 40, 42, 52, 80, 93
Normandy Invasion, 123
Noyce, Bob, 135
Nvidia, 133

Oliveira, Nathan, 91
opportunity costs, 141
optogenetics, 118
outsider perspective, 111

Packard, David, 21, 132, 133, 134, 146–47
Page, Larry, 105, 109, 132, 135
patents, 106
Patterson, Dave, 33
pay cuts, 68
PayPal, 136
Percy, Walker, xi
Perlman, Itzhak, 137
personal computers, 2–3
PhD students, 55
Pollock, Jackson, 91
Porras, Jerry, 134
protests, 73–76
public speaking, 17–18, 69–70, 72–73

Q&A sessions, 28

radiology, 60
rankings, 5, 111
reading, 119–20
Reduced Instruction Set Computer
    (RISC), 32–33, 103
regenerative medicine, 14
reputation, 38
Rhodes, Cecil, 127
Rhodes Scholars, 6, 127–29
Rice, Condoleezza, 4, 34
Rice, Susan, 128
risk-taking, 76–82, 84, 88, 150; aversion to,
    140; in business vs. academia, 102–3
robots, 60
Rockefeller, John D., 14
Rockefeller Foundation, 14
Rockefeller University, 14
Roosevelt, Franklin D., 121
Roosevelt, Theodore, 21, 121
Rothko, Mark, 91

salary freezes, 67
San Francisco earthquake (1906), 132
Santa Clara County, Calif., 70
Sarbanes-Oxley Act (2002), 30
saying no, 24–25, 40–41, 56
scandals, 38, 129, 141
Schmidt, Eric, 105
search engines, 104–5
Sedol, Lee, 118
self-driving cars, 60
service, xi, 6, 35–49, 140
service learning, 46–48
severance, 68
sexual assault, 75–76
Shakespeare, William, x
shareholders, 30, 38
short-term thinking, 26, 37–38
Shriram, Ram, 133, 156
Silicon Graphics, 3, 12, 13, 14
slavery, 32, 144
smartphones, 104
Socrates, 22
South Africa, 47
Spence, Michael, 128
Spilker, Jim, 133
Stanford, Jane, 42–43, 46, 143
Stanford, Leland, Jr., 42
Stanford, Leland, Sr., 42–43, 143
Stanford Challenge, 27–28, 111, 113,
    131–32, 141, 148
Stanford Charter School, 43–45, 62, 110
Stanford Industrial Park, 132
Stanford Initiative for Innovation in
    Developing Economies (Seed), 47–48
Stanford Linear Accelerator, 112
Stanford Teacher Education Program
    (STEP), 53–55
Stanford Telecommunications, 133
Stanford University: Anderson Collection
    at, 92, 147; Bing Concert Hall, 137–38,
    147; Business School, 47; Cantor Art
    Museum, 147; Computer System
    Laboratory, 3; Denning House, 130,
    146, 153; Education School, 45, 54;
    Electrical Engineering Department,
    1, 3; Engineering School, 4, 33, 133,
    142–43; founding of, 132; McMurtry

Art Building, 148; Medical School, 45;
    start-ups linked to, 108, 132–33
Stanton, Edwin, 144
start-ups, 19–20, 103–8, 132–33, 134
Stein, Isaac, 19, 92–93
stem cells, 13–15
storytelling, xi–xii, 7, 127–38
strategic planning, 110–15, 131
student housing, 91
student protests, 73–76
Sullivan, Kathleen, 112, 113
sweatshops, 75

teacher training, 53–55
teamwork. See collaboration
technology transfer, 106, 108
tenure, 25, 26
Terman, Frederick Emmons, 132, 146
Terman Engineering Scholastic Award,
    142–43
Tesla Motors, 135–36
Thiebaud, Wayne, 91
Thirteenth Amendment, 32
Tilghman, Shirley, 72
time horizons, 26, 37–39, 102
Titan (Chernow), 14
To Kill a Mockingbird (Lee), 51
Transcontinental Railroad Act (1862), 144
trust, 30, 93
truth-telling, 23–25
Turing Award, 33
Twain, Mark, 73
two-pizza rule, 86

Uber, 103
underemployment, 60
undergraduate admissions, 57
undermatching, 57
unemployment, 60
unions, 75
University of California, Berkeley, 32
University of Chicago, 154

Varian Brothers, 132
venture capital, 12–13, 105, 106, 107
Very Large Scale Integration (VLSI), 3
Vietnam War, 121, 123

Volkswagen, 7, 129
Volpe, Mike, 156
volunteering, 11, 40–41, 90, 93, 98

Washington, George, ix, 14, 21, 23, 122
Wells Fargo, 7, 129
Wilson, Woodrow, 145
women in the sciences, 71–72
Woolsey, James, 128
WorldCom, 7
World War I, 145
World Wide Web, 2–3, 13, 104

Yahoo, 104, 132, 133
Yang, Jerry, 132, 133, 156
YouTube, 111